MIME

Richmond Shepard

MIME

The Technique

MIME
of Silence

An Illustrated Workbook
Illustrated by E. M. Louise Sandoval

Drama Book Specialists (Publishers)
New York

Sections of this book appear in the Los Angeles and San Francisco
Light Opera Associations Musical Theatre Workshop's
manual for the performer in musical theatre.

Library of Congress Catalog Card Number: 72-134993

ISBN 0-89676-008-1

Printed in the United States of America

0 9 8 7 6

To Phillip Schrager, my first teacher, who started all of this;

and

To my wife Hadria, who puts up with all of this.

MIME

WHAT IS MIME ABOUT?

MIME AND THE PERFORMER

Mime teaches the theatre performer to communicate physically as well as vocally. Performance in theatre demands skill in developing full characterizations including the character's walk, physical behavior, and general physical presence, as well as clear and expressive gesture. Many actors can't move and can only communicate vocally; most singers are notoriously stiff. With the study of mime, performers learn to be physically relaxed on the stage, they learn to gesture, and they experience the basis of the kinds of characterization that the varied situations in all theatre demand. They learn economy of movement: when to gesture, and when to remain still. And, they learn to project a large clear image; this is vital, particularly in the large theatres of today.

The aim of all mime technique exercise is to gain control of every separate part of the body in every possible direction, so that whatever movement one wants to make can be made, whatever physical posture is necessary for a character can be sustained, whatever physical image in space is necessary can be performed.

THE LANGUAGE OF MIME

Mime (or pantomime, the words mean the same thing) is communication by gesture. It can be communication of an idea, an emotion, a story, but it is never the acting out of words. It should not even use verbal concepts, only physical concepts. For instance, if an actor points to another actor (signifying "you"), and then beckons (signifying "come"), and then points to the ground in front of him (signifying "here"), he is behaving verbally. He is literally acting out words. For him to communicate physically, all he need do is beckon, which tells the "you, come here" story more economically. If an actor wants to communicate to an actress that he loves her, he must neither mouth the words "I love you," nor would he point to himself ("I"), point to his heart ("love"), point to her ("you"). As a mime, he would communicate his love by the way he looks at her and behaves toward her, not by acting out words. The language of the mime must be universal so that practically anybody on this planet can understand his story. Mouthing the words "I love you" would not be understood in France or China, but a look of love, and behavior and responses with the feeling of love in it would be understood anywhere.

Objects

The mime uses no sets, no props, no devices. His only means of communication is his own body, driven by his ideas and emotions: This body must be trained, skilled, taut, flexible, supremely expressive. It is his instrument, his tool, his keyboard, his canvas and paint. If he needs a chair, he creates one out of air, and sits on it as if it were real; if his story calls for a ball, or a tennis racquet, or a stove, or a tall hat, or an egg, or a locked door, or a heavy weight, or anything else, he creates them, gives them substance and the illusion of reality, without any real object being present. Ability to handle imaginary objects will be of use to most actors in most plays. While it is true that you will generally be handling a real coffee cup or whiskey glass, the substance in it will not be whiskey—it will be tea or syrup in water. The actor must, with his imagination and skill in handling the imaginary, turn it into what the script calls for. When Othello has to strangle Desdemona, he must create an imaginary Desdemona whose neck is a sixteenth of an inch larger than that of the actress portraying her. He must strangle that imaginary neck with all his strength and energy as if it were real, while the actress who plays Desdemona pretends to die. His physical skill and control will be vital to the performance. In addition to this kind of situation, there are actually imaginary props in many plays: windows between the actors and the audience that must be opened, imaginary doors, and so forth. Most actors handle them badly, and instead of creating the image, destroy the illusion. Their windows wobble, they forget to let go of doorknobs, etc. Mime training teaches you how to use imaginary objects, and in addition, your awareness of how objects should be handled gives more clarity to your handling of real objects.

Mime, Acting and Dance

Mime is acting in stylized form. It is not a dance form. It demands real emotion, concentration, and motivation. The concern of the mime while performing is the same as that of the actor, not of the dancer. In dance the plot is the framework on which to hang the form. The story is the vehicle for the display of the technique. So, in terms of his story, the dancer is concerned with the questions "Where am I going?" and "How shall I get there?" He asks, "Shall I go from upstage right to downstage left?" and if so, "Shall I leap, run, twirl, skip, slide, roll, spin, etc.?" It is the form that is most important. The audience wants to see giant leaps, marvelous balance, extraordinary grace; they want to see the human figure go beyond itself, outdo itself, extend itself. They want to see beautiful form; the story is really of secondary importance. The actor is concerned with plot and character. His questions are, "What am I doing?" and "Why am I doing it?" He is primarily involved with his motivations, with conveying the story, with the character's intentions and actions, and not with physical form. The form, in this case, is the vehicle for the display of the plot, the framework on which to hang the story.

The mime is concerned with physical form only while he is in the classroom. He practices his techniques over and over until they become second nature to him, and then, in performance, he is to disregard them and concentrate on the acting problem: "What am I doing?" and "Why am I doing it?" He will, of course, use all the techniques he has been practicing, since we must not forget that he is limited to physical communication alone, and cannot speak. But if he becomes concerned with technique while performing, his performance will be external, superficial, and will not move the audience. So the mime is an actor who moves, not a dancer who acts. Mime is a kind of stylized acting, rather than a kind of "theatre-dance."

Projecting the Physical Image

The mime has only his body to tell his story; he has no amplification, no loud-speakers; he must project the image with only his physical being. There are several things a mime does to make this image clearer to his spectators. First, he magnifies all his actions: his gestures, movements, physical reactions, must be just a bit larger than life size. But these larger reactions cannot just be imposed from the outside. As in all acting, the motivations behind the actions must be justified emotionally; then, after really feeling, really experiencing the reactions of the character he is portraying, the mime builds on this base of reality, and magnifies. He doesn't "portray" an emotion—he doesn't define it in the air; he experiences the emotion, and magnifies the result. Otherwise the audience won't believe him, and if they don't believe him, they won't care.

Second, he must complete each gesture before beginning the next one. He must separate his actions, in fact, each part of each action. In rehearsal he would, for instance, first raise his arm, then stop, lower his hand to his pocket, stop, put his hand in his pocket, stop, take out a key, stop, bring the key to the keyhole, stop, insert the key in the lock, stop, turn it, stop, open the door, stop, and so on. He practices his actions this way, with sharp clear movements, strong impulses, and square corners. In performance, he rounds out the corners, smoothes out the actions so that the stops are not really noticeable, but they are, in some subtle way, still there.

A third thing the mime may do is to wind up for each action. That is, before making a downward gesture, he would first move his arm in the opposite direction a bit, thereby making the downward gesture bigger, and more easily seen. Before reaching forward, he would bring his arm back a bit, then forward. Winding up makes for bigger movement, and thereby greater communication, and it also provides a more flowing, more graceful gesture, which is more beautiful to watch; and while our main concern is communication, we do not dismiss beauty.

The effect of magnification, separation, and winding up is a kind of stylization that enables people in the back of an auditorium to see more clearly what is happening on the stage. That is its primary purpose: to be seen. If the resulting movement is graceful or beautiful, we may consider it a bonus.

CONVENTIONS

There are several long-time conventions in the mime technique. In this silent art, there are some sounds that the mime may make on the stage: he may make the sounds of objects, never of people. He may tear an imaginary piece of paper, and make a tearing sound with his mouth; he may knock on an imaginary door and make a knocking sound with his mouth or by stamping his foot on the floor. But when he laughs or cries or sneezes, he does it silently. Actually, the proper way for a mime to cry, is for him to be wearing water-soluable eye-liner under his eyes, and when the tears roll down his cheeks, they dissolve the make-up, which streaks down his face, showing the tears clearly to the spectators. If the tear stops exactly seven-eighths of an inch below the left eye, and five-eighths of an inch below the right eye, that would be perfect. But just do your best.

A mime tries not to touch the other actors on the stage with him. If he must kiss a girl, he does it from half an inch away, and it is as if the air around the girl is a part of her: this gives a kind of magical effect. We may take someone's hand if necessary, but a push, or a blow, or a kick are accomplished without actually touching, and the recipient behaves as if he were actually struck. Timing is important here, since any anticipation of the blow will destroy the illusion. Actually, this should be applicable to all theatre; we are, after all, only representing events, not living or behaving them, and actors should never be so out of control as to actually hit another actor. We may want the illusion of reality on the stage, but we certainly don't want reality itself.

A mime should never repeat a gesture, unless he does it in some other way. He should never point twice or beckon twice. He should do it one time, big and clear: To repeat it would only be redundant. If he must beckon more than once, he might first use one finger, then perhaps his hand, and then his thumb or his whole arm. This same principle holds true for spoken dialogue in a play; if the words are repeated, they must be said differently each time, or they are redundant. Same principle for words in a song.

TRAINING THE BODY

The physical technique of mime works toward gaining control of each separate part of the body, and of the body as a whole. The main divisions are: the head separate from the neck, separate from the chest, separate from the waist, separate from the pelvis. The unique separations are the isolations of the neck and the waist. I know of no dance form in any culture on this planet that isolates the waist, and the kind of neck isolation we do is only approached in Eastern dance forms. So the head, neck, chest, waist, and pelvis are moved separately in many directions until each piece is controlled and usable. When the isolated movement of the chest is achieved, the chest is used as the impulse-source for moving the arms: the chest is tilted, the energy-flow extends down the arm, moving it like a lever, and then reaches the hand. Later the impulse may originate in the pelvis, flow to the chest, and finally motivate the arm movement.

The mime practices achieving control of his hands, and of the separate joints of each finger. This work gives clarity to all hand movements, whether the performer is handling real or imaginary objects. He exercises the muscles of his face—not because there is any set expression for an emotion, but because the more physically flexible and expressive his face is, the larger and clearer will be the projection of the emotions he is really feeling on the stage. He practices using his body as one rigid piece, as a unit, as well as breaking it into pieces; he becomes like a wooden doll, with the legs acting as a system of levers, and nothing changing but the placement of weight and the legs. He practices using just his eyes to tell a story. The eyes are supremely expressive on the stage, and most actors neglect them. When looking about on the stage, it is much more dramatic to turn just the eyes rather than the whole body, or even just the head and neck, but you rarely see this done. Once one has practiced communication with the eyes alone, a new communicative tool is present that can be utilized when needed. The mime trains **all** of his body, so that no matter what the story he wants to tell, he is able to do it. This kind of physical control and expressiveness gives greater dimension and depth to any performance.

THE ILLUSIONS

A mime can give the illusion of walking, while actually he remains in one spot; he can appear to run, while covering no ground; he can appear to be climbing a ladder or a flight of stairs, or walking a tightrope, or pushing or pulling heavy objects, or leaning on a fence, or having a tug of war, or riding a bicycle, or rowing a boat. He is alone on the stage: no props, no scenery, nothing but himself. These illusions are not practiced to be exhibited by themselves, but because a character in a sketch may have to do any of them in the course of the story that is being told. They are an excellent means of developing coordination, and are fun; you get to mystify your friends once you have mastered a couple of them.

SENSE MEMORY

The mime uses sense memory in the handling of all of the imaginary objects that appear in his stories. That is, he must remember what the real object looked like, felt like, smelled like, sounded, or tasted like, and he must recreate it as if it were real. If he picks up an imaginary bottle, it must have and maintain the shape, weight, texture, etc., of a real bottle. He must use all the muscle tension in his hand that he would need to handle a real object. He must open his hand bigger than the bottle, and then close it onto the bottle to grasp it, and he must let go of it when he is finished using it, and has to be careful that his hand doesn't drift through the bottle once it is back on the table. If he creates a table, he must not walk through it. Any physical objects created on the stage must not be violated; it must be related to as if it were real. If the mime is eating a meal, the more he can smell and taste the imaginary food with his imagination, the more real it will be to the audience. If he is supposed to be looking at a building, or a ship, or anything else, the more **he** can visualize it the more vivid the image to the audience. Obviously this has a direct correlation to any theatre performance, since the scenery is never real and the chicken is made out of plaster. Mastery of imaginary objects can only make the handling of real ones clearer.

BECOMING AN OBJECT

There is an advanced concept of handling objects, and that is projection into the object, actually becoming part of it, or the object itself. If one were sweeping with an imaginary broom one would become part broom, and perhaps the leg and foot would do the sweeping, while you grasped the imaginary handle. You might bring your knee up to your chest with your lower leg pointed to an opponent, and use the leg as a gun, pulling the trigger on your calf, and punching the foot forward on each shot. You might become a ball that bounces, a pair of scissors, a washing machine, or perhaps even a piece of bacon frying in a pan. When doing these things, we try to capture not only the physical action of the object, but also the attitude the object might have if it were conscious. The washing machine could react to the dirty clothes that are put in it, and might sneeze when the soap powder is poured into it.

ANIMAL CHARACTERIZATIONS

The mime practices animal characterizations in order to do human characterizations that have animal characteristics. He practices being an animal; he tries to find as many things as he can that the animal does, as many mannerisms as possible; he tries to create the face, and, most important, he tries to find the attitude of the animal. Then he evolves his animal up into a person who has similar physical mannerisms and attitudes. For instance, he might be a cat: What does a cat do? It lifts its shoulder at each step, it stretches, it washes its face with its paw, it hits at a piece of string, it crouches, it licks its mouth, it pounces, etc. The animallike person would do the same things, modified, upright. The washing of the face might become a little gesture of wiping the mouth, the attitude would have to be catlike. If you were doing a birdlike character, he might look around sharply, he might be fluttery, he might scratch his chin with his shoulder, and so forth. These animallike characters can be applied to characters in a play; used to make the characters interesting and alive. This is a most valuable tool for characterization for any kind of theatre.

FALLS

Part of the mime technique is to practice falling, so that if you have to fall in a show, you will be able to do so without hurting yourself. There is no reason for anyone to be injured falling on the stage, and many characters have to die, or faint, or trip in many shows. We also practice limping, staggering, and being drunk, so that they become part of the performer's vocabulary, and can be called upon when needed.

ECONOMY OF GESTURE

The mime practices using a minimum of effort in his performance; he economizes, conserves his energy. This does not mean he performs small—his performance is large, but he eliminates all extraneous movement, and only performs the minimum necessary to tell his story. He always takes the simplest path. When he moves one part of his body, the rest of it remains still, until needed. It is as hard to learn not to move as it is to learn to move. This same principle holds true for athletes: When a professional football player finishes a game, he is very tired, but he is not wiped out; when an amateur athlete finishes a strenuous game he is completely wiped out; when a professional actor finishes a really strenuous show he is very tired, but he is not wiped out; when an amateur actor finishes a strenuous show, he is wiped out, completely exhausted. The amateurs have not conserved their energy, their strength.

The simple gesture is more dramatic: If the entire body is still and just the eyes are turned, or if just one finger is moved, all focus is on the one small movement, and it is quite dramatic. If the body is moving around, several parts moving at once, and the eyes turned, nobody will notice, and the movement will be lost. Turning just the eyes is even more dramatic, and, believe it or not, the turn of the eyes will be seen by the person in the last seat in the top row of the balcony in the largest theatre I have seen.

MIME AND WORDS

If narration is used, the mime should **not** suit the action to the word. That would be redundant. He should use gesture that goes beyond the word, shows other aspects not included in the words, or which communicates something different from the words, so that the audience will receive the combination, which should be more than either the words or the actions separately. The narration might say "Once there was a little girl . . . . " The action has to show what kind of a little girl, what she does, how she behaves and relates to others, what her attitudes are, what her peculiarities are. If the narrator were to say, as the character, "I think I'll go," and the actor at the same time pointed to his chest, pointed to his head, pointed to his chest again, pointed off stage, he would be doing charades. In mime, if the narrator said, "I think I'll go," the mime might start for the door, come back and have a piece of pie, start for the door again, come back and kiss the girl, pack a lunch, look back at the girl, and trip over the doorsill. This same principle holds true for gestures while singing. The singer who points literally to parts of his body as he sings about his heart, his mind, and points up for the sun and offstage for the girl, is not only redundant, he is corny. Or worse, in a serious song, funny. The gestures while singing should be relaxed, natural, simple, and in context with the character and situation, but should not repeat the words. If you do a gesture that means the same as the words, however, it should usually come before the word, not after, since gesture is stronger than words on the stage.

THE MIME

The mime, using his body as his tool, his imagination as his motivating force, and his talent as his fuel, creates a whole world of characters and scenes on a bare stage. He can portray a man catching butterflies if he chooses, or he can portray man's humanity or inhumanity to his fellow man if he chooses. He can make observations of human behavior, or he can advocate social change: Whatever he wishes can be communicated. The physical technique is just the beginning. Anyone with a normal amount of coordination can learn the technique. Then it is up to the talent, the imagination, the artistry of the performer. One can learn the basics of the technique in a year; to become an artist takes, just as in any other field, many years of constant work and practice.

Mime has been compared to ordinary acting as poetry is compared to prose. A mime can, with a single gesture, convey a world of thought and emotion, just as a line of poetry can convey what might take a chapter of prose. Even take the prosaic mime gestures that everyone uses: a thumb raised in the air to hitch-hike, Churchill's "V" for Victory which has now become the Peace symbol, or the raised middle finger of the insult. All convey a world of meaning with a single gesture.

For the theatre performer, the enlargement and clarification of the physical image that is projected from the stage is vital. The study of mime technique is the most efficient method of acquiring control, simplicity, and strength in the physical part of the performance. This does not take the place of dance training, which is also vital for the performer. Mime training is more concerned directly with physical characterization, clarity of gesture, and convincing physical portraiture.

A BRIEF HISTORY OF MIME

A number of years ago, when I first decided to write a book on mime technique, a publisher said he was interested in the idea only if I did an extensive chapter on the history. I spent six months in the New York Public Library doing research, looked at every book on every primitive culture I could think of, every book on the Commedia dell' Arte, every book on theatre history, Greek theatre, Roman theatre, Hindu theatre, Chinese theatre, French theatre, and English theatre in the place. I started writing the chapter according to my view of the world at that time—this was before I became the mystic I am today. At that time I was a materialist who believed in economic determinism, and I organized the chapter into: "Mime Under Primitive Communal Systems," which included the early cavemen, the American Indians, the Eskimos, many tribes in Africa, South American Indians, Australian Aborigines, natives of New Guinea, and others; "Mime Under Slavery," which included the Ancient Egyptians, the Greeks, the Romans, and others; "Mime Under Feudalism," which brought us into European theatre and the Commedia, Javanese and Balinese theatre, and others; and finally "Mime in the Modern Western World," with a further note on mime as an offshoot of dance and as an offshoot of comedy.

Rather than go into vast detail in this book, which is really supposed to be only about the technique, I'll just give you some of my conclusions. Every primitive culture had mime as part of its religious ceremonies and as part of its entertainment participation events. The primitive early caveman probably danced about what he was going to do on the hunt, and then, when he returned home, enacted what had actually taken place. The cave drawings in southern France and northern Spain indicate this, and the pattern is repeated in all primitive cultures—the acting out of events, real or hoped for, is universal in the history of man. As man became more sophisticated, the dramas became more complicated, and included propitiation of the gods, legends, myths, history, and finally, mere entertainment.

There are few primitive peoples without a war dance, and the pattern has usually been: Challenge, Pursuit, Conflict, and Defeat. Sounds like lots of today's movies. These people also tended to imitate nature around them, and animal characters were performed by many primitive mimes: the American Indians with their Eagle dance, the Balinesians with their Monkey dance, the Australian bushman miming the baboon, or a swarm of bees, etc. Most of these people also did harvest dances, and weather dances.

The drama of the Orient is all based on mime: Hindu dance is simply gesture-language which has been stylized into an abstraction of the original literal form, but can be understood by anyone with only a minimum of exposure; Siamese dance is similarly based on mime, and Japanese Kabuki remains essentially a mime theatre; the Peking opera was a mime theatre, but unfortunately its skills are being lost since the recent conversion of its traditional forms to a political theatre. Most of these Oriental theatre forms portray stories and legends about Gods or great heroes in movement, sometimes accompanied with a text that is sung.

The ancient Egyptians probably had some kind of a mime theatre, and it was probably religious. It is from the Greeks, however, that the mainstream of modern mime can clearly be traced. Before the performance of the tragedies, it was common for the actors to do a mime show as a kind of introduction. The principal mimes were called Ethologues, which means painters of manners, and they tried to teach moral lessons in their work. In addition, farces and other such clowning were performed. During the plays, the choruses were miming as they spoke, and reacting with physical movement to what occurred. Aristotle mentions mimetic dances in his descriptions of these plays. The Greeks also had the Pyrrhic dances, which were a kind of military pantomime: one showed a fight with shields, another was a battle against shadows, and another depicted single combat.

There is a rumor that most of the Greek mimes came from Sicily, and another that Livius Andronicus, a Greek, first did pantomime in Rome. Whichever, it seems that Emperor Augustus of Rome liked pantomime, and it thrived under his reign, even though most of the mimes were slaves. The subjects of the Roman mime performances were probably based on mythology, and if you are familiar with mythology you'll know that there was plenty of room for adventure, tomfoolery, and anything else. There was sometimes an offstage speaker during these performances, but the players themselves did not speak. It may be noted that mimes were condemned by the early Christian writers because of their lewd conduct and revealing costumes.

The Roman Empire split, and the Eastern half, centered in Constantinople, became the cultural center. When the Roman Empire fell, the Eastern area became the repository of its culture, and when Constantinople fell to the Turks in the fifteenth century, the mimes fled, traveling throughout Europe.

Meanwhile, back in the West, the Church, from the tenth century on, began to accept theatre, instead of condemning it, and actors now began to do Mystery and Morality plays with religious themes, many of these in mime. They did stories from the Bible and lives of saints, and moral problems of common people, first in the churches, and later in private theatres, in streets, and in parks. By the time the Byzantine mimes returned from Constantinople, the Italian theatre was as vulgar as it was religious, and out of this union grew the Commedia dell' Arte.

The Commedia was an improvised theatre wherein the actors played stock parts, with variations in the scripts—like today's television soap opera series. The shows were improvised, and were full of mime and visual schticks which they called Lazzi. If you are really interested in this theatre, there is a good book called **Commedia dell' Arte,** by Pierre Du Chartre, and another by him called **Italian Comedy,** which I would recommend.

We can see from Shakespeare's **Hamlet** that mime, which was probably brought there by the Romans, was very much in evidence in England. It was continued there by John Rich in the early seventeen hundreds and later, at the end of that century, by the most famous English mime, Joseph Grimaldi, a brilliant satirist. By the early eighteen hundreds pantomime in England began to change, gradually growing (or deteriorating, depending on your point of view) into its present form, which is musical theatre, with mime, singing, dancing, and speaking.

In France, during the beginning of the eighteen hundreds, a mime developed who is still a great influence today. Perhaps you have seen the French film which is a fictional biography of him, called **Les Enfants du Paradis** ("Children of Paradise"). His name was Jean Gaspard Batiste Debureau, and his theatre was called The Funambules. Debureau changed mime from slapstick to theatre: he did stories with plots, with character interaction, with contemporary meaning. He chose to play the character of Pierrot, instead of the traditional leading-man, Harlequin, and his theatre was successful until the early 1840s. After Debureau's time, mime in Europe became a secondary art form, although it survived as part of an actor's training, and occasional mimes were found doing performances in theatres and night clubs.

The real father of modern mime is Etienne Decroux. He studied at the Vieux-Columbier school of the theatre in Paris, under Charles Dullin, in the early 1920s, became interested in dramatic movement and in mime, and then did the research that lead to the modern technique. He practiced, formulated exercises, created illusions, and eventually taught. Decroux is a great theoreti cian, but never had the charisma that is required for a star performer. His students, however, fulfilled his dream. Jean-Louis Barrault performed the role of Debureau in **Les Enfants du Paradis,** and went on to become France's greatest stage performer. In that film, Decroux plays the role of Debureau's father. And Marcel Marceau, a French Jew, finally spread Decroux' message over the world.

The basic difference in the performances of these three men is this: Decroux, in performance, shows the technique. Each move is done separately and individually, each action spelled out. You become engrossed in the skill of physical movement, the perfection of each gesture; but you do tend to forget the story, and eventually the exhibition may become dull to the ordinary theatergoer. I, of course, found it fascinating, as would any mime, but I don't advocate it as a way of communicating with an audience. Barrault does stories in mime, and his work is directly related to that of Debureau, who he played in the film. He uses several characters in his stories, and generally does period pieces. I find his work moving and beautiful. Marceau is, I feel, the greatest mime in the world at doing his particular thing, which is—Showing How a Man Does Things. He shows how a man rides on a train, or catches a butterfly, or tames a lion, or he portrays the various characters you'd meet in a park. His eye for the foibles of human behavior is brilliant, and the nuances he captures ring with a universal truth that has never failed to capture his audiences in any country. Most of the other mimes I have seen use Marceau's technique. They try to emulate him, and show how a man does things, but no one does as well as he. A few have developed their own style, but most have not only copied Marceau's style, they have even acquired his personal movement habits.

In America today there are several mimes—Tony Montanaro, who was in my company in 1953 or '54, is in New York doing excellent work. He worked in France and Italy in 1956 and '57, and has his own style. Paul Curtis in New York directs The American Mime Theatre. Paul was a student of Decroux, and has developed his own personal approach to mime which he calls "American

Mime." Rusdi Lane is in Los Angeles. Several Israeli mimes have toured the United States, and two of them make their home in New York: Solomon Yakim and Juki Arkin; and Claude Kipnes is now making his home in this country. Bernard Bragg, a deaf and dumb mime, is now working with the Theatre of the Deaf. Ron Davis, in San Francisco, has stopped performing mime, even though he calls his troupe The San Francisco Mime Troupe. They do a kind of hip contemporary minstrel show, and are famous for being busted for obscenity. Actually, all protest theatre is obscene to the Establishment, so they are really being arrested for their rebel ideas, rather than for their language.

Most night clubs in Europe have mime acts in them, and Decroux' students, and the students of his students, are all over the world. Poland has a national Mime theatre, which does very strong athletic mime, with generally somber themes, and Czechoslovakia has the Prague Mime Theatre, which recreates a kind of Commedia feeling, and leans to comedy. Both of these marvelous troupes tour the world, and get rave reviews everywhere except in New York, where, if you're not exactly like Marceau, you tend to get blasted. They have mostly one frame of reference there, and deviation is not tolerated.

My own work tends to be in the line from Debureau through Barrault, to today. I do stories with plots and characters that are about contemporary themes: war and peace, man's relationships with his fellow man, love, etc. And, in the tradition of the Romans, I sometimes use offstage narration for some of the pieces. I always use live music with my performances. Recorded music can't be used well—the timing may be different from night to night, and a laugh may hold up a moment for varying lengths of time.

I must, of course, mention the great mimes of film: Chaplin, who influenced Marceau tremendously, Keaton, W. C. Fields, Stan Laurel, Harpo Marx, Harold Lloyd, and others. They found their techniques through necessity, but all tended to adhere instinctively to the mime technique obligations.

Many contemporary comedians are natural mimes, like Red Skelton, who has carried it further than anyone today, Jerry Lewis, Sid Caesar, Adam Keefe, Zero Mostel, Dick Van Dyke, George Hopkins, Frank Gorshin, Richie Pryor, Jackie Gleason, Lucille Ball, Jonathan Winters, Flip Wilson, Guy Marks, and most of the impressionists, like Rich Little, Dave Frye, and George Kirby. And finally, there have been dancers, like Mata and Hari, Angna Enters, and others, who found mime as an offshoot of dance.

Mime seems to be spreading today, probably mostly because of the television appearances of Marceau. Hopefully, this trend will continue.

A WARNING

Before you undertake the study of mime, you should be warned—there is very little market for it in America today. People always want me to teach it, because it's good for actors to be able to move well, but if you want to be a mime, you should consider it very seriously before entering it as a profession.

I'll give you a few examples of what to expect: When I auditioned for the Ed Sullivan Show, the man in charge said, "It's too . . . too . . . quiet." I said, "Yes. It's mime." They said no. When I auditioned for the Joey Bishop Show, they had told me that they didn't want any mime on their show, so I said I was a comedian. I did my mime act, and when I finished, the producer said, with a look of distaste on his face, "That's . . . mime." I said, "Yes." They didn't hire me. Steve Allen's producer let me do theatre games on the show with Geoff Edwards and Stefanianna, but wouldn't let me do mime. At U.C.L.A. I was told that they don't want any mime shows, don't want to see any, and wouldn't consider hiring a mime—they are only having Marceau this year because another artist canceled. Mime won't make them any money.

You can expect this kind of rejection as part of the natural course of being a mime, so most mimes give it up. Alvin Epstein is a fine actor today, but doesn't do mime. Rusdi Lane has been working with The Committee, and doesn't do mime. Hamilton Camp is a comic actor and a singer today, and does no mime. So think twice, and then think again before you pick this profession which is unknown and unmissed in America. The work itself is rewarding and gratifying, but it's hard to find places to work. So if you become a mime, you may end up being a mime teacher, which is a different thing, or you may end up using it as part of something else. As for me, I wouldn't give it up, but I always was a Don Quixote.

THIRTY LESSONS IN MIME TECHNIQUE

The proper costume for a mime class can be tights and a leotard for the women and tights and a T-shirt for the men; actually, anything form-fitting that allows free movement is acceptable, such as shorts or old levis, or, in warm weather, even a bathing suit. For the feet, soft canvas acrobatic slippers, modern dance shoes, very old ballet slippers, or socks can be used. The sole must be thin and very flexible, and preferably all in one piece, so that it is easy to go to the half toes. New ballet slippers have too stiff a sole. Bare feet don't slide enough, and so are not acceptable, and tennis shoes are too stiff.

The mime class should start with a physical warmup; this can be dance exercises, calisthenics, or anything including bending, stretching, twisting, and pliés (deep knee bends). The purpose is to stretch and tone the musculature before doing the control exercises of the mime technique.

The warmup should be five to ten minutes, and the optimum time for the entire mime class is about an hour and a half; or if the class is crowded, perhaps an hour and three quarters.

Do not face a mirror while doing the mime exercises; if you do, you will later imitate what you saw, rather than feeling what to do. You may check yourself at a mirror, but then work away from it.

LESSON ONE

Discussion of basic principles of mime; the double-zero position; diaphragmatic breathing; inclinations; rotations; transtations; transtation improvisations; facial exercises; imaginary objects; walk #1.

This first class can start with a discussion of some of the general principles mentioned in Chapter One: the universal gesture idea, magnification, separation, winding up, the conventions, etc.

The Double-Zero Position: We start all mime exercises from what we call the double-zero position. It is: Stand erect, heels together, feet at a ninety degree angle, tuck your pelvis under (as if two pins were coming at you, one aimed at your waist in front, and the other aimed at your lower buttocks in back), lift your chest without pulling your shoulders back, and get your head level (as if a string were pulling the back of your head upwards). The arms and neck should be relaxed, the knees straight. It is a stylization of a normal standing position.

Diaphragmatic Breathing: Mimes, actors, singers, and dancers should breathe from the diaphragm while performing. For the singer it gives breath support; for the mime, it enables him to keep his chest lifted when he wants to. There are many characters, such as Frank Butler in **Annie Get Your Gun,** who must maintain a lifted chest for the two and a half hours of a show. The only way this is possible is to breathe from the diaphragm, without the chest rising and falling at each breath. The diaphragm is just below the bottom ribs; it should be thought of as a kind of balloon: When you breathe in it inflates, when you breathe out it deflates. The chest stays lifted, and just the area around the diaphragm moves while breathing. Practice this until you can do it easily. Since the chest must be lifted for the double-zero position, it includes breathing from the diaphragm. Breathing must always be silent, no matter how strenuous the performance—practice keeping a clear air passage while panting.

The inclination and rotation exercises are the basis of the technique, and are the ones that separate the body into the five pieces: head, neck, chest, waist, and pelvis. They are done in several directions.

The Forward Inclination: Stand in the double-zero position, and lower the chin, tilting the head forward as far as it will go without moving the neck. The neck is still perpendicular. Stop. Then incline the neck forward, keeping what you already have with the head. Relax the back of the neck, and let it go as far forward as possible. Stop. Next tilt the chest forward, breaking at the bottom rib, and without collapsing the chest or bringing the shoulders forward. The shoulders maintain their relationship with the chest, and the waist is still vertical, with the pelvis still tucked under. The head and neck are still continuing forward, and should not relax yet. Stop. Next incline the waist forward as far as it will go, keeping the pelvis tucked under. Do not lose any of the other forward inclinations that you have already achieved. Stop. Now relax the pelvis, and tilt it as far forward as it will go. Be sure you don't relax the other inclinations. You should now be rolled forward as far as the body will go, with the knees straight and the weight on the toes. Stop. Now come up one piece at a time: First the pelvis straightens by tucking under tightly, then the waist lifts until it is vertical, and then the chest lifts all the way up with the shoulders down, then the neck lifts, and finally the head straightens, and you are back in the double-zero position. Do this sequence slowly and carefully three times.

18   *Forward Inclination*

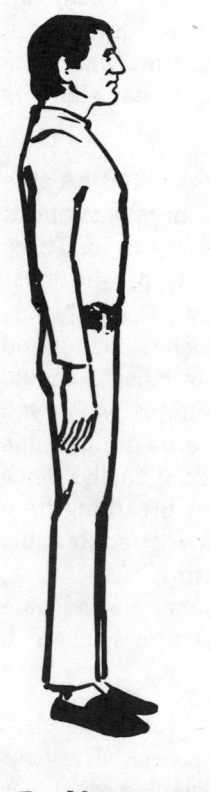  

1. Double-Zero Position   *2. Head*   *3. Neck*

4. *Chest*   5. *Waist*   6. *Pelvis*

The Rear Inclination: Step forward onto the left foot, and settle the weight evenly between both feet, with the left heel about a foot or a foot and a half in front of the right toe. Do not turn out either foot, and keep the pelvis pointed flat forward. Lift the chin, inclining the head toward the rear, and keeping the neck vertical. Stop. Incline the chest to the rear, breaking at the bottom rib in the back. This is a small move, and should catch in the small of the back. The head and neck continue back. Next tilt the waist back until you feel it catch at the waist, and finally, for the inclination of the pelvis to the rear, just bend the back knee as far as you can, without bending the front knee, and keep the rest of what you have achieved. Stop. Be sure you don't sink in and collapse the chest when you do the pelvis. Keep the inclinations you have achieved. Then come back up, one piece at a time: First straighten the knee, bringing the pelvis up, then the waist, then the chest, then lift the neck, which should bring the head into its first lifted position, and then lower the chin, and you are vertical again. Do this slowly and carefully on each side: first with the left leg in front, and then with the right.

20

Rear Inclination

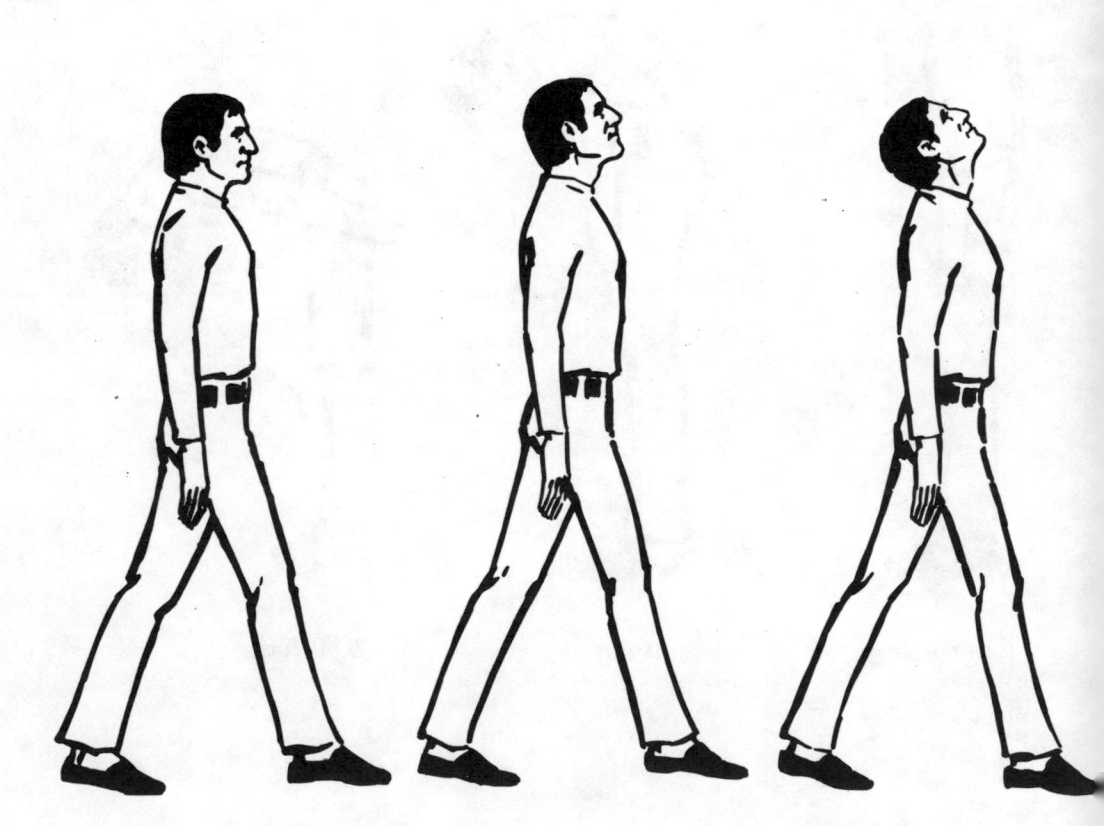

1. Double-Zero Position   *2. Head*   *3. Neck*

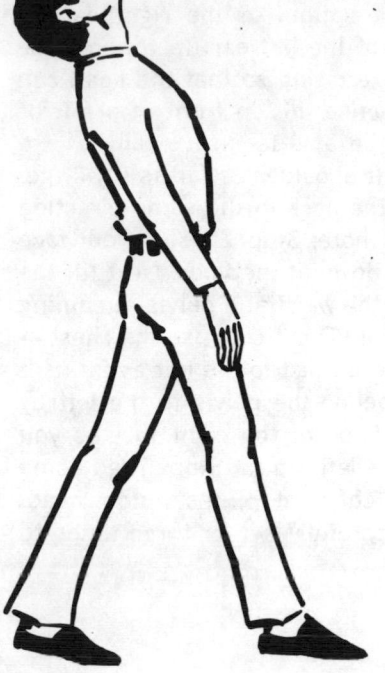

4. Chest

5. Waist

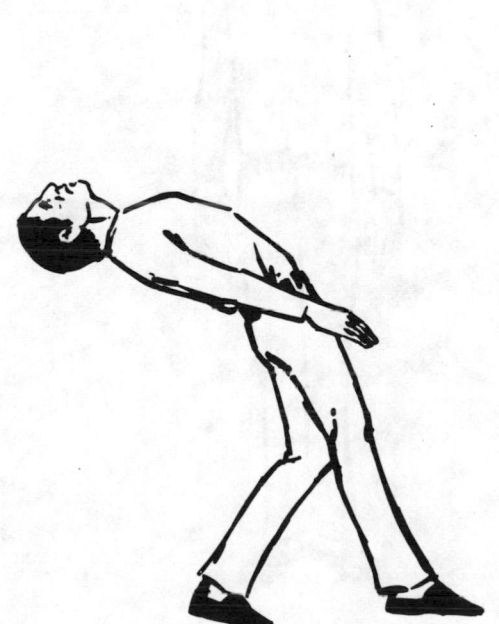

6.

The Side Inclinations: As a preparation for this, place the palms together over the head with the elbows open. Now reach the bottom of the right ear up towards the right elbow; then reach the bottom of the left ear up towards the left elbow. This starts the muscles in the neck exercising so that the head can move back and forth like a Hindu dancer's. Practice this in front of a mirror every day for a few minutes, and you will soon be able to do it easily.

After the preparation, tilt the head toward the left shoulder as far as it will go, with the neck remaining vertical. Stop. Now tilt the neck in the same direction until you feel it would tilt the shoulder to go any more. Stop. Be sure your face remains facing straight forward, and not looking down at the floor. Next tilt the chest to the left, breaking at the bottom rib, with the waist and pelvis remaining vertical, and the head and neck continuing on down. Don't collapse the chest—keep it lifted as you incline it. Stop. Now incline the waist to the left as far as it will go without moving the pelvis, and finally, incline the pelvis to the left by bending the right knee, and going onto the half toe of the right foot as you tilt over as far as possible to the left, pushing the left hip in. Stop. Then come up one piece at a time: pelvis, stop, waist, stop, chest, stop, neck, stop, head. Now do it to the right. Practice this slowly and carefully two or three times to each side.

22

Side Inclination

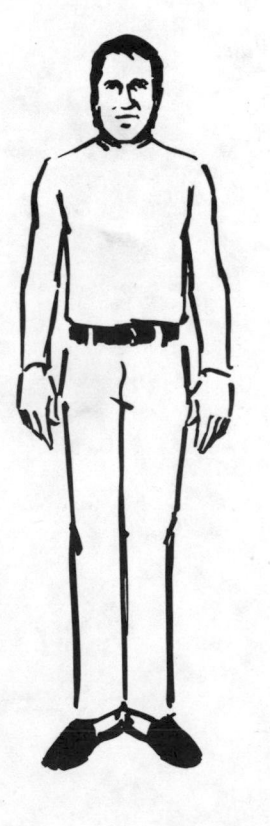  

1. Double-Zero Position   *2. Head*   *3. Neck*

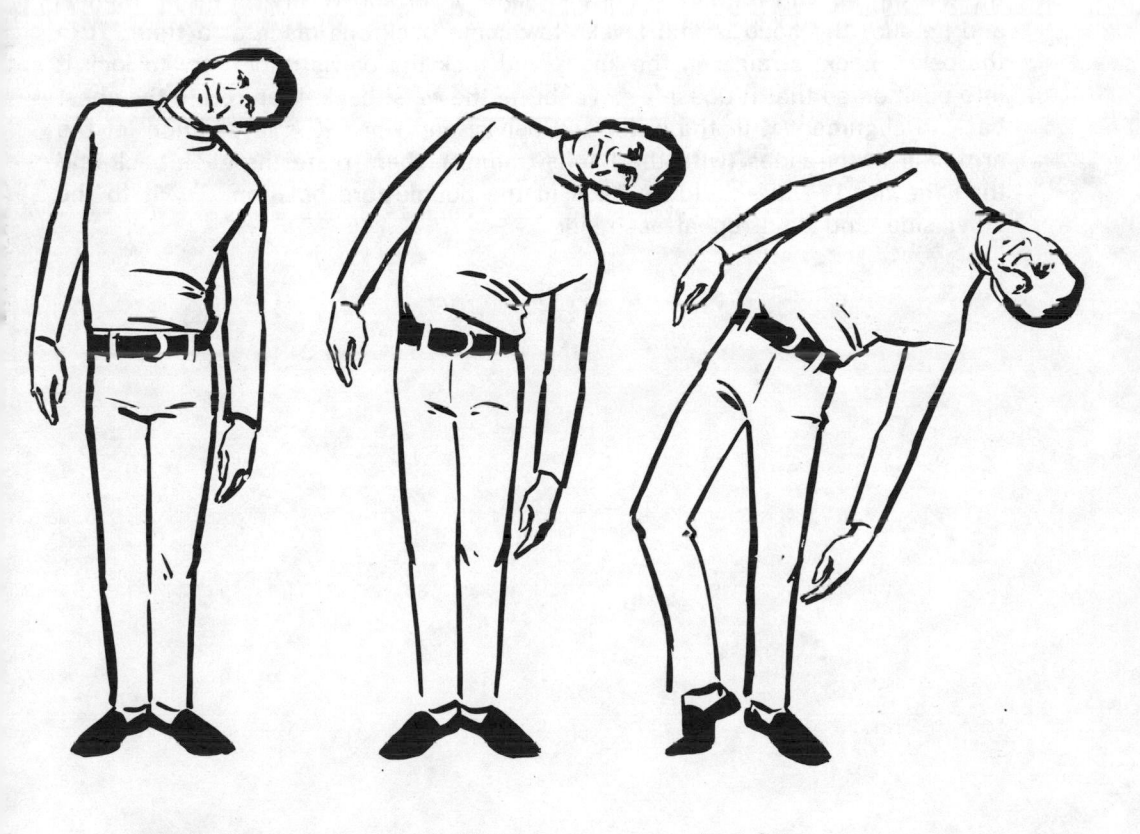

4. *Chest*   5. *Waist*   6. *Pelvis*

The Rotations: As a preparation for this, extend the arms out to each side as if you were hugging a giant barrel, keeping your hands below shoulder level. Now let your arms drift up and down with the palms down, as if you were standing in water, and as if the water were offering resistance, so that your hands trail behind your arms: you break at the wrist, and your hands droop up as your arms come down, and the hands droop down as the arms drift up. From now on, whenever you put your arms and hands down, let the hands trail a bit.

Once again, start in the double-zero position, and turn the head to the left, keeping it vertical, until the big muscle on the right side of the neck starts to pull. Stop. Rotate the neck to the left as far as it will go, and keep the head turning. The head must be kept level. The head will usually be level when it feels like it is leaning toward the front of the room. Stop. Now turn the chest to the left, with the head still leading, pulling to the left. The instant the chest hits its final position in its turn, at the point where the waist would turn, stop the movement of the chest and allow its impact impulse to knock the arms into the air into an open position, as if the big barrel you were hugging is now a bit off to the left. Extend the hands as if you were reaching to shake hands. Stop. Twist the waist around to the left as far as it will go without turning the pelvis, and without changing the relationship between the arms and the chest. Stop. Now, to turn the pelvis, rotate it, and bend the right knee, go onto the half toe of the right foot, keeping the heel over the spot that it leaves. Keep the left hip in, and the entire body straight, level and vertical. Pull up higher, and be sure the head is still level. Now come back one piece at a time. Turn the pelvis back, straighten the knees and tuck the pelvis under, try to lock it into position so that it doesn't move; bring the waist back, then rotate the chest back to alignment with the waist and pelvis, and when it is in position let the arms fall to the sides (with the hands trailing), then rotate the neck back and then the head. You should be back in the double-zero position. Try it to the other side, and then repeat each side.

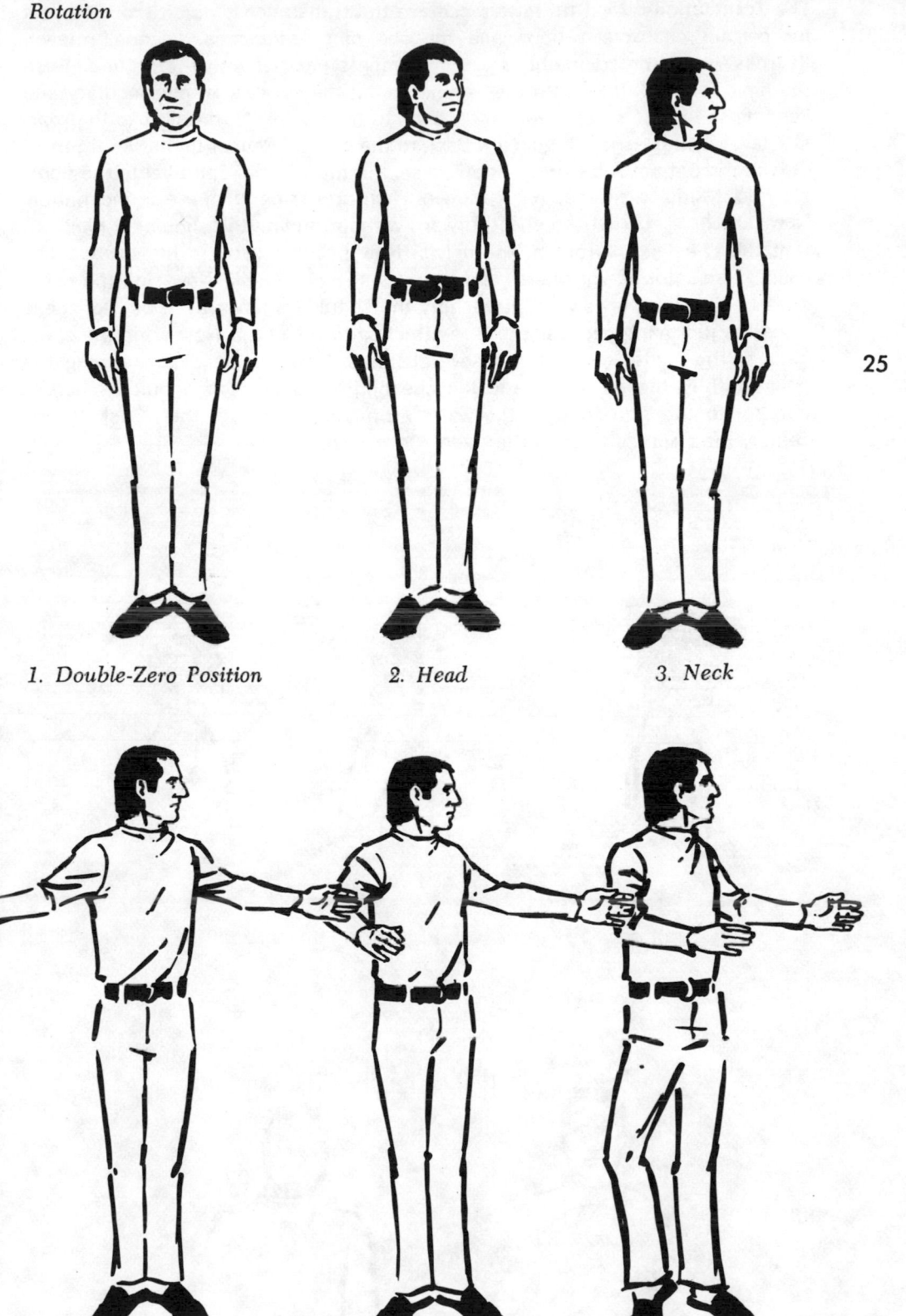

1. Double-Zero Position 2. Head 3. Neck

4. Chest 5. Waist 6. Pelvis

The Transtations: Next in importance are the transtations, which are the basis for certain characterizations and for one of the illusions. "Trans" means "across," and the transtations are movements parallel with the ground. Push the head forward, level with the ground, using the neck as an intermediary and keeping the chest still. Now bring it back to the center. Now pull it to the rear, still level, as far as it will go. Now back to the center. Repeat this several times. The chin must not raise or lower on these, but must remain parallel to the floor. Now do it side to side, as we practiced when preparing for the side inclination. Now the chest: Thrust the chest forward without pulling the shoulders back, so that the chest is in front of the pelvis. Now bring it back to the center. The waist is an intermediary here, and the pelvis remains still. Now sink the chest back behind the pelvis without pushing the shoulders forward. In both of these the arms just hang because they are attached to the chest. Now bring the chest back to the center. Repeat this several times. Now side to side: Keeping the pelvis tightly tucked under and the chest lifted, slide your shoulders across parallel to the ground with the waist as an intermediary, then back to the center, then across to the other side. Do it several times.

Head Transtations

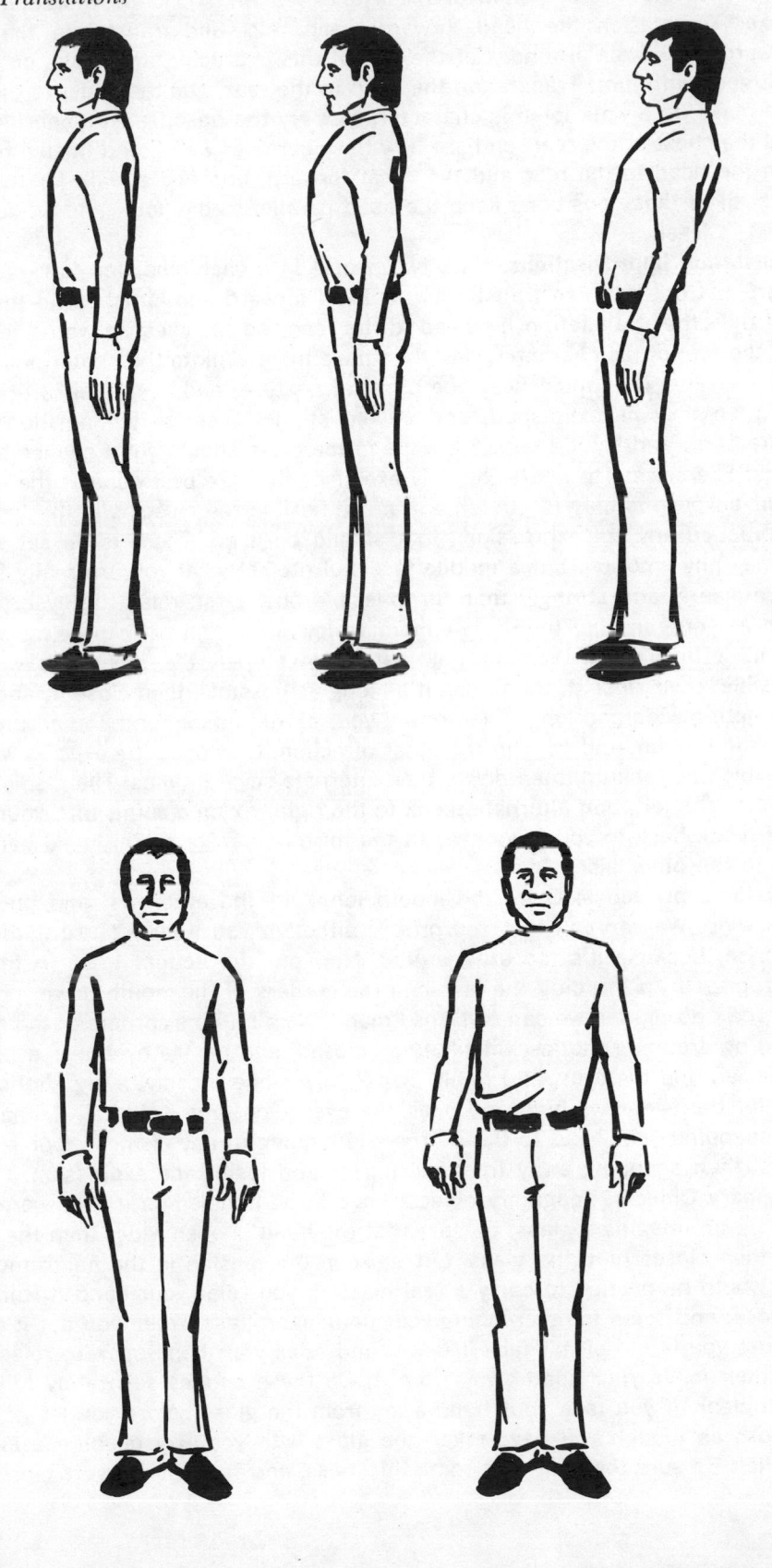

Now let's combine a couple of these and see what kind of characters they make: Transtation the head forward; keep this, and transtation the chest forward. Now walk around: Get the feel of this character, and make up a walk that goes with him. Transtation the head to the rear, and the chest to the rear, and make up a walk for this character. Now try the head transtationed forward and the chest to the rear, and see how this character walks; and finally, transtation the head to the rear and the chest forward, and find a walk for this one. With all of these positions keep the head parallel to the floor, and be sure the chest is level.

Transtation Improvisations: Have two people face each other ten to twenty feet apart. Let one of them transtation his head forward and his chest to the rear, and the other transtation his head to the rear and his chest forward. Let each get the feel of his character, and then have them walk to the center and meet, and interact. They must keep the physical posture, and base their attitude on it. When they have finished, and walked off, let them switch positions (and characters) and try it again. Everyone in the class should get a chance at this.

Facial Exercises: These are the only exercises that are best done at the mirror. Their purpose is only to stretch and make flexible the muscles in the face, not to practice any set expressions that should be used. There is no set way to display any emotion, but a mobile face will project what you are really feeling more clearly and strongly than an inflexible one. First, raise the eyebrows as high as you can, and then lower them as low as possible. Keep going up and down, letting the movement get faster. Next open the mouth as wide as possible, then close it, then open it as long as possible, then close it, and keep alternating wide and long. Then rotate your closed lips around and around in a chewing motion, and do it in the other direction. Now open the eyes as wide as possible and look up, then down, then alternate several times. Then look to the right, to the left, and alternate. Look to the right, fix on a point, turn your head to it. Look back to your own eyes in the mirror, then bring the head back. Do this to the other side.

Now for expressions: Open the mouth long, lift the eyebrows, and open the eyes wide. We can call this "surprise," although you wouldn't use it to show surprise, because it's too exaggerated. Now put the bottom teeth in front of the top teeth, protruding the jaw, pull the corners of the mouth down, pull the eyebrows down, and we can call this "mad." Next pull the corners of the mouth down by dropping the jaw with the lips closed, and lift the eyebrows a bit and squint around the eyes, and think "sad." Now smile broadly, a big idiotic grin, and lift the eyebrows high and open the eyes wide, and we'll call it "happy." Try snapping your head to the mirror and landing in any of these four expressions, then snapping away from the mirror and losing the expression.

Imaginary Objects: Imaginary objects have to be handled as if they were real. Pick up an imaginary glass; be sure that the hand is open wider than the glass and then closes onto the glass. Lift it; keep the tension in the hand and arm that would be needed to carry a real glass. If you relax your hand it will start to close, and seem to be crushing your imaginary glass. When you put it down, be sure you let go of it: Place it down, and relax your hand open to release it, and **then** move your hand away from it. Do these actions separately to make them clear. If you take your hand away from the glass before you let go of it, it looks as though you have taken the glass with you. Try opening a kitchen cabinet: Be sure the knob has some thickness, and that your fingers close onto it. Be sure the knob retains its level above the floor as it opens the door. Be sure you let go of it before taking your hand away from it. Then close it. Practice. Have each member of the class practice handling an object, and then have them perform their object for the class.

Walk #1: This is a stylization of a normal walk as you walk down the street. In a normal walk there are two processes that take place: first there is a shift of weight, and then there is a change of the leg and arms. We will separate these two moves as we do our version. Stand with the right foot pointed forward with all the weight on the back foot; the left arm forward, the right arm back. There is no weight at all on the front foot: The toe barely touches the floor. Move 1: Shift all the weight onto the front foot. Don't change the arms at all, and be sure that **all** the weight is now forward. Move 2: Change the leg and the arms—that is, now point the left leg forward, without putting any weight on it, and at the same time put the right arm forward and the left arm back. That's it. Those are the two moves of the walk. Now continue it: Shift the weight forward (be sure the arms don't change as you shift) then change the leg and arms (be sure no weight goes to the front foot on the change). On the change, turn the toe over, bring the arms in close to the body, the knee in close, and keep the toe on the floor. Continue across the floor, and try it a few times back and forth.

Homework Assignment: Practice handling an imaginary object, and bring it in to show at the next lesson.

Walk #1

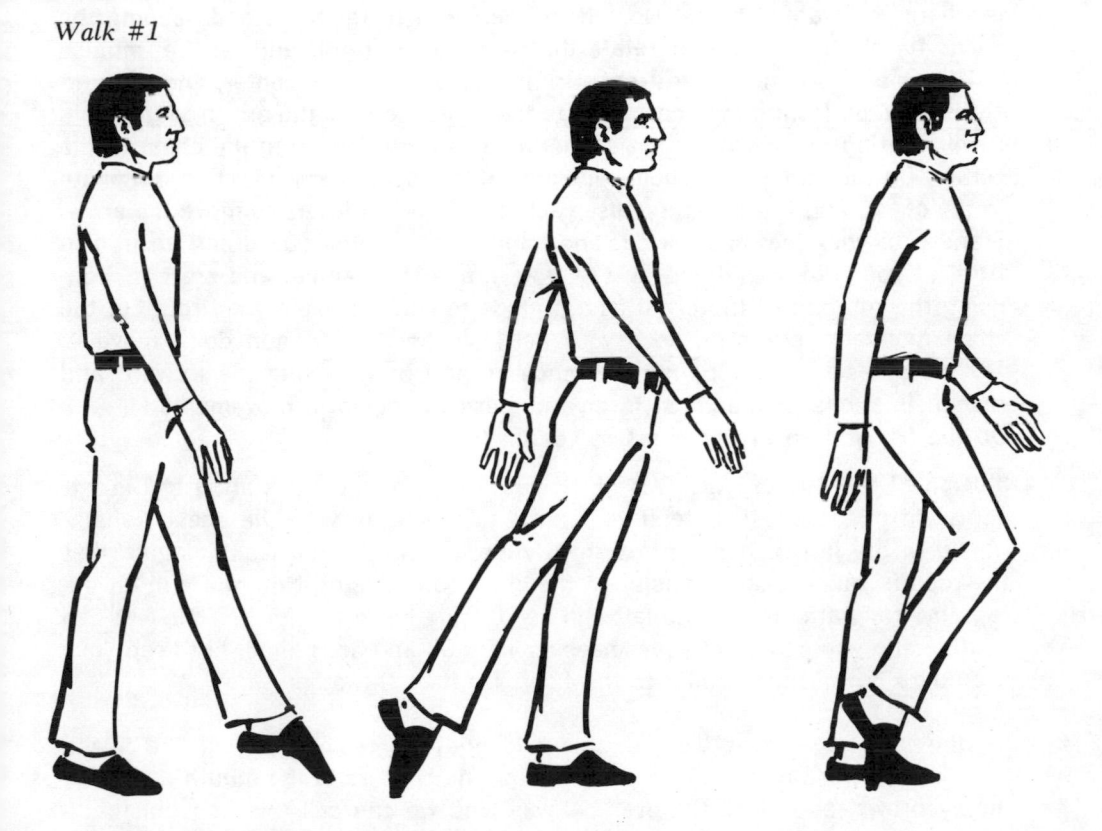

1.   2.   3.

Inclinations; rotations; chest impulses; transtations; the illusion of the tug-of-war; facial exercises; slow motion exercise; walk #1.

In this lesson begin by repeating the forward, rear, and side inclinations, and then the rotations.

The Chest Impulses: Rhythmically incline just the chest forward, then center, then rear, then center, and repeat several times. Then incline the chest to the right, to the center, to the left, to the center, and repeat this. Then rotate the chest to the left, to the center, to the right, to the center, and repeat. Now: Incline the chest to the left, and when it hits the end of its tilt, let the impulse flow through the right arm, so that the leverage from the inclination lifts the right arm. Bring the chest to the center, and the arm stops lifting. Incline the chest to the right, and the right arm will lower as a result of this impulse. Do this several times, and then do it with the left arm. Now try lifting the left arm forward, in front of you, by giving it an impulse from a rear inclination of the chest, and lowering it with a forward inclination of the chest. Do it several times with each arm, bring the chest back to the center position when the arm is where you want it to be. Now lift the left arm to the side, and keeping the pelvis tightly tucked under, rotate the chest to the right, and let the impulse pull your arm around to the front. Bring your chest to the center, and the arm stops moving. Rotate the chest back to the center to stop the arm from moving; it will continue in the direction of the impulse until you bring the chest to the center. Do the other arm. The movements of the arm, in any direction, originate in the chest, and the chest impulses act as a series of levers to move the arms. Stand with your feet apart a bit, and imagine an ironing board and an iron in front of you. Put your hand on the iron, grasp the handle, and start to iron, using the rotation of the chest as a prelude to each stroke of the iron: Let the chest motivate your arm; keep your pelvis tucked under, and don't move it. Try the other arm. Try painting a fence up and down, using the forward and rear inclinations of the chest to give impulse to your arm movements.
Do the transtation exercises as in Lesson One.

Illusion of the Tug-of-War: This illusion is based on the transtation to the left and right of the chest. Extend your arms to the right, with the chest transtationed to the left. Grasp an imaginary rope in your hands. Now imagine that the rope is yanked, and transtation the chest to the right. Now **you** pull on the rope by transtationing to the left and keep going back and forth. Your feet can shuffle, and you can bend your knees as you pull and are pulled, but keep your shoulders down and parallel to the floor. Do it to the other side.
Practice walk #1 again.
Do the facial exercises we did, and add one expression: stretch the space between the nose and the upper lip, pulling the corners of the mouth down, lift the eyebrows, and close the eyes halfway, and we can call this "snobbish."
Perform the imaginary objects that were brought in for homework.

30

Slow-motion Exercise: Have two people stand upstage facing the rest of the group, several feet apart. Place two imaginary tables downstage, one opposite each of the people. The two walk as slowly as they can to the tables, being careful to put their feet down as slowly as they lift them. On each table is an imaginary bowl of cherries; they must each eat a cherry, and throw the pit at the other person. All reactions must be in slow motion, time must be allowed for the pit to go through the air, and both must be hit by a pit, and should react to it. Slow motion action makes you finish each action before you begin the next. If it's a large group, several can do this exercise at a time, each throwing 2 pits at 2 other people.

Homework Assignment: Bring in an imaginary object that you handle using a chest impulse to motivate each arm movement. Do it slowly and carefully with square corners. For instance: Incline the chest to the rear, lifting the right arm until it is over your head, bring the chest to the center, which stops the arm movement. Grasp an imaginary glass on the shelf. Incline the chest forward, lowering the arm until it is table height. Bring the chest to the center, and the arm stops. Put the glass on the table, let go of it. Incline the chest forward, dropping the arm to the side. Bring the chest back to the center. Be sure you stop after each movement.

LESSON THREE

Hand exercises: pointing, beckoning; exercise on hunger and appetite; eye improvisations.

Hand Exercises: The purpose of the hand exercises is to provide strength and clarity to hand movements and gestures. To begin, warm up the hands by opening the hands as wide as possible, and then closing them tightly, alternating quickly, until you can't do it any more. Next, put the fingertips together, lift the elbows high, and try to bend the fingers backwards, stretching all the knuckles. Now, open the palms wide, and face the hands straight forward. Touch the index finger to the palm and allow this movement to pull the next finger down to the palm, pulling the next one, etc., until they are all closed. As you close, try to keep the hands open, so that they stretch, and keep your thumb open. Now turn your closed hands over, and open them one finger at a time, index finger first, allowing each finger's action to pull the next one smoothly. Now turn your hands back to the open facing forward position, and repeat it many times. Try to keep your hands closed as you open them, and open as you close them, so there is tension.

Now try the opposite: Start with your hands open wide, and extended in front of you, palms up. Close the little finger first, as if you are grabbing something, and allow each finger to pull the next closed; the thumb stays open. Now turn your hands over, wrists up, and open little finger first, almost like you are describing two balloons in the air. Then palms up again, and close again, etc. Repeat this many times.

1. Index Finger   Hand Exercise

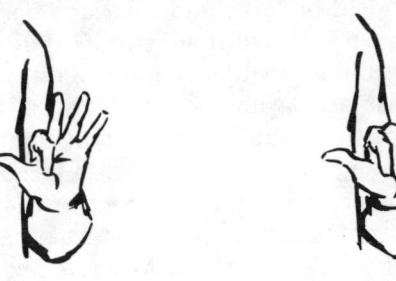

2. Little Finger   Hand Exercises

Pointing—there is no one way to point; the following is a way among many, whatever is right for the character and the situation is the one to use. All pointing should be large and clear and done only once, never repeated, unless you point in a different manner. Lift your elbow to the side so that it is level with your shoulder, and have the lower arm pointing straight up at right angles to the upper arm, with the hand closed, and the index finger extended in a pointing position. Straighten the arm without moving the elbow, so the finger is now pointing. Be sure the wrist is locked and remains straight in line with the arm. Repeat this point with each arm, and then do it to the front. Now take the same starting position, but with the hand open, and the edge of the hand facing what you will point to. As you straighten the arm, close the fingers one at a time starting with the little finger (just as we practiced when exercising the fingers), all except the index finger, which points. The thumb is closed, and the wrist doesn't break. All should be closed by the time the arm is half-way straight, and the final pointing is done with the finger and arm. Do it with each hand, and in several directions, always starting with the edge of the hand facing what you will point to.

34

Pointing

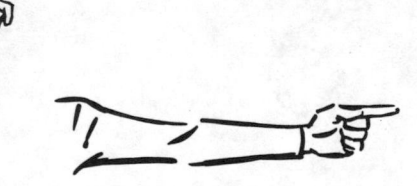

1.   2.   3.

Beckoning—push the palm towards what you will beckon, and as the elbow straightens, close, in turn, the little finger and the next two, closing the thumb on them, and drop the wrist back as you turn the arm over. The elbow is straight, the index finger is extended, and the wrist is bent back toward the floor. That is move 1. Move 2 is to bend the elbow and wrist into a beckon. Do it several times with each arm in several directions.

Try first pointing, and then dropping the wrist back, and then beckoning. Try extending the beckon so that you end by pointing to the ground in front of you. There is no one way to beckon: You can do it any way you wish; but it must always be large and clear, and done once.

Beckoning

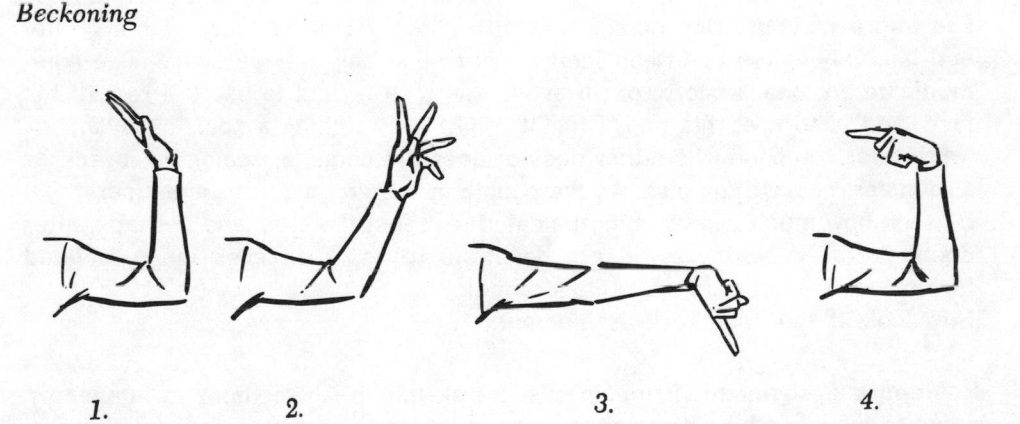

1.   2.   3.   4.

Exercise on Hunger and Appetite: This exercise is one of the most useful concepts in acting. First, without discussion, each member of the group should perform his own version of hunger, and his version of appetite. He should not say which he is doing first, nor should there be any guessing until everyone has done his. There should be no eating in any of these improvisations: only the physical expressions of hunger and appetite differentiated from each other. By the time all have done them, a pattern will probably be seen to have formed. Hunger is in the stomach: It is an inner organic emptiness that needs to be filled. Appetite is in the eyes and the mouth. Hunger has to do with a **need;** appetite with a **want.** Most plays are concerned with the needs and wants of its characters. Most characters are involved, on an inner level at least, with their needs and wants. Now, have a girl stand in the center of the stage area, and have one of the men in the group feel hunger for the girl, walk to her, and, without touching, say some line of dialogue that has no relationship to his feeling. The girl is to remain indifferent. He is to feel an inner organic emptiness that only she could fill, while he says something like, "I went to the store and bought two yellow bulbs and two blue ones" or "Uncle Jed has gone over the hill again." Then let him try the same line of dialogue while feeling appetite for the girl: walk to her, perhaps look her over, and say the line. They are two different scenes, and neither of them has anything to do with the words that are said. Now have them switch places, and let the girl do the exercise with different dialogue. Each member of the group should do each part. There are many scenes in plays where this kind of thing takes place: where there is talk going on, but the scene is really about the relationship between the two people and their feelings for each other; such as when the young man meets the princess in **Call Me Madam** and they argue about the Grand Dutchy of Lichtenburg, they are really needing each other, feeling hunger for each other. This exercise, if applied to scenes, can give dimension to the performance.

Repeat the Facial Exercises: All five expressions we have done so far.

Eye Improvisations: One person sits in a chair, facing the rest of the group, and back about ten or fifteen feet. He is to use only his eyes, and is to communicate an idea, a story, or an event. He is to try not to use the rest of his face, and is to keep his body still. It might be watching a sporting event, or waiting for someone who either does or does not come, or seeing an insect, or a monster, or anything else. As the people in the group do this exercise, it will be seen how much can be communicated with just the eyes, and perhaps, after doing it, the performers will not be afraid to use their eyes in an isolated fashion on the stage. It is quite dramatic.
Now look at the homework assignment.

Homework Assignment: Bring in a short sketch in which there is hunger or appetite for something or someone, and in which, at some point, something is communicated with just the eyes.

36

LESSON FOUR

Inclinations; rotations; chest impulses; transtations; tug-of-war; first illusory walk; facial exercises; improvisation #1; slow-motion exercise; duets.

Repeat the inclinations, the rotations, the chest impulses where the chest moves the arms, the transtations, and the tug-of-war. This time, in the tug-of-war, allow the elbow to bend and the knees to bend, shifting the weight back and forth.

Illusory Walk

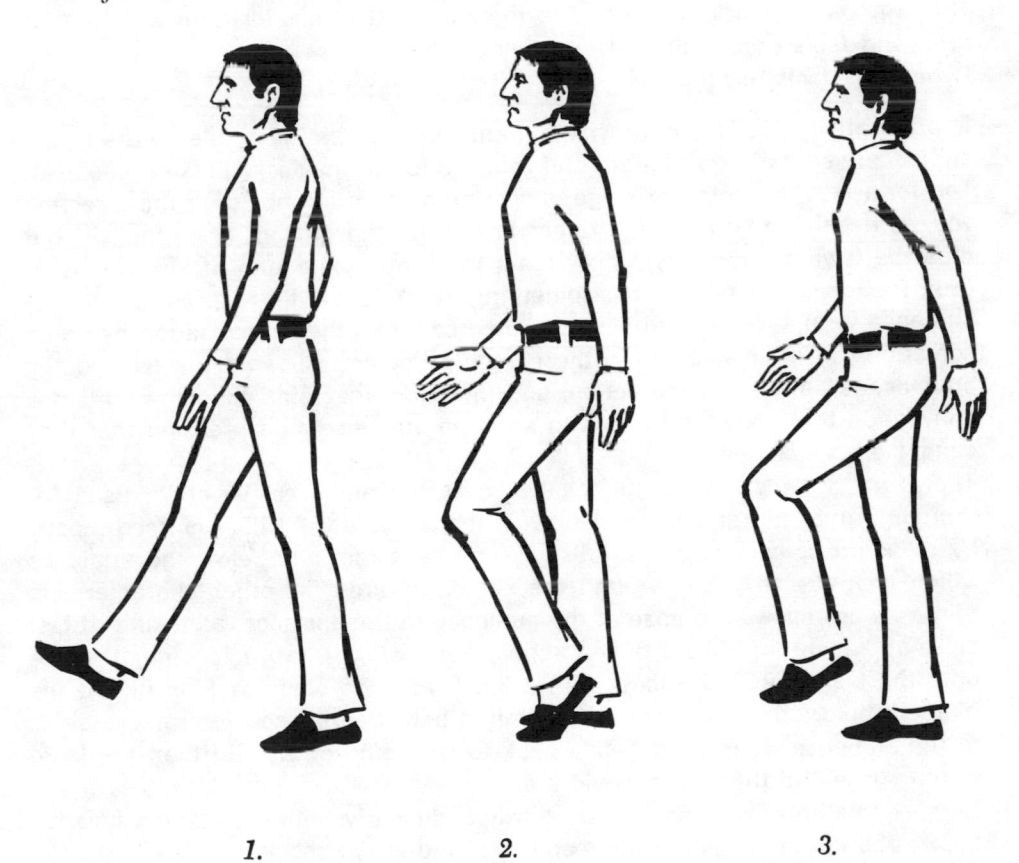

1.   2.   3.

First Illusory Walk: This walk gives the appearance of walking, while the performer actually stands in one spot. It should be practiced in two halves, and then the halves can be put together to make the walk. Start with the right leg extended into the air, foot flexed, and knee straight with the heel about twelve or fourteen inches off the floor and with the left arm forward, the right arm back, hands below waist level, and the elbows rather straight. Now, as you pull in the right leg and put the foot on the floor, bend the left knee and go to the half-toe of the left foot; as you bring the right leg in, swing the right arm forward, and the left one back. Repeat this move from the starting position over and over. Then do it on the other side, with the left leg swinging in as the left arm goes forward, and going to the half-toe of the right foot. These are the two halves of the walk. Now to complete it: Start with the right leg extended, left arm forward, pull in the right leg, going to the half-toe of the left foot, and right arm going forward as before, ending with the right foot on the floor next to the left one, as before. Now, without moving the arms, lift the left foot into the air, from the half-toe, and extend it forward, with a kind of bicycle-peddling motion, until the knee is straight, and now you're in the start of the other half of the walk. Pull the left leg in, going to the half-toe of the right as you change the arms and put the left foot down. Now lift the right in the circular motion, keeping the arm still, and keep going. The hard part is: Keep the arms in place while you lift the foot, and only change them when the leg pulls in straight. This will keep them in opposition to the knee that comes forward; it is hard at first, and feels unnatural, but becomes easier.

Repeat the facial exercises.

Improvisation #1: This improvisation embodies several principles; gaze at the audience, separation of action, and relating to an imaginary person or object. The form is: Walk onto the stage, stop; see a person or object in the direction you were walking (it can be straight ahead, on the ground, or in the air, but must be toward the wings), stop; react to it with some kind of an expression (not the ones we practiced—something real), show the expression to the audience, bring your head back, and then continue the improvisation by doing something to or in relation to the person or object. Showing the face to the audience is not part of the action, and the body freezes as you show it. It is a convention that you may do this to show an audience an expression that they cannot otherwise see.

There are three gazes in the theatre: over the audience, which is used for thoughts, images, remembrances, etc.; at the audience, which is used mostly by stand-up comedians, or M.C.'s, or for the aside; and below the audience which includes all gazes around the set or towards the other characters. In mime we are allowed to gaze at the audience in this instance, as a kind of fast close-up which is not part of the action. For instance, two actors might come onto the stage, one advancing with a knife, and the other backing up. At the moment before the knife strikes they might both freeze, show their expressions to the audience, snap their heads back toward each other, and then the knife would strike and the victim would die.

Be sure this improvisation is done slowly and clearly, with each action finished before the next is begun. Each member of the group should try this.

Do another slow motion exercise, this time with imaginary bananas on the table; peel and eat them, and throw the peel at the other person.

Look at the homework assignment.

Duets: Two people face each other, ten or fifteen feet apart, and walk to the center, passing each other. They turn, and one of them (assigned by the leader) will start the scene, the improvisation. He can start with a character relationship or an object, or a place, and the other person must go along with what is happening, and take his character, attitudes and actions from what the originator sets up. There is no talking in this. For instance, one student might sit in an imaginary chair, and motion for the other one to file his nails. The other one must then become a manicurist, and the scene proceeds from there. Or one may look at the other with adoration, and ask for an autograph by extending an autograph book and pen. The second person must now become a movie star, or a celebrity of some kind, and should accept the relationship that the first person established. This can go anywhere, and should not be limited by reality. One hint: Avoid conflict in all improvisations. Go with what is happening; agree rather than conflict. Conflict ends the scene; if you go with what is happening, it can go on, and you will find more things to explore. When it is over, have the two people switch roles, the one who followed will now originate another scene, with the former leader following. Let as many people in the group do these as there is time for.

Homework Assignment: Bring in a short sketch with all movements motivated by chest impulses, and in which at least one object is handled.

The body as a unit: forward and side tilts; unit knee bends; scale-fulcrum tilts; sways; walks; being drunk; improvisations with the body as a unit.

In this series of exercises the body is used as one rigid piece, and the only things that change are the legs and feet, and the weight; from the head to the pelvis the body is kept tightly in line in one piece, as if it were made of a piece of wood.

40 **Tilts:** Keep the double-zero position, and tilt to the right, keeping in line with the left leg, and trying not to break at the waist. Do not keep the top half of the body upright—keep it in line with the rest. Now tilt back to the center, and then to the other side.

Side Tilt

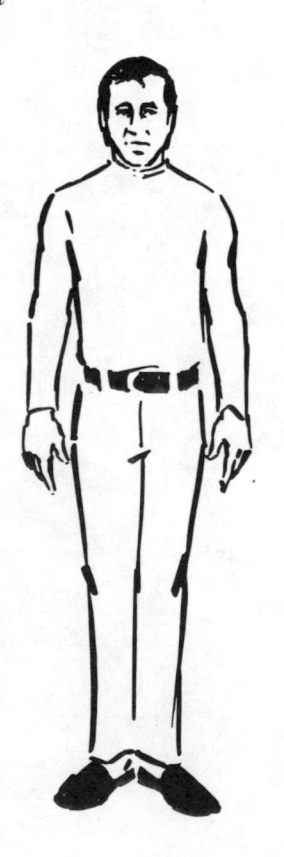

1. Zero Position

2.

Close the toes until they are three inches apart, and open the heels about an inch, but otherwise maintain the double-zero position. Now tilt forward and back, being sure not to break at the waist. The head will tend to remain upright: don't let it—the whole body, in line, should tilt forward.

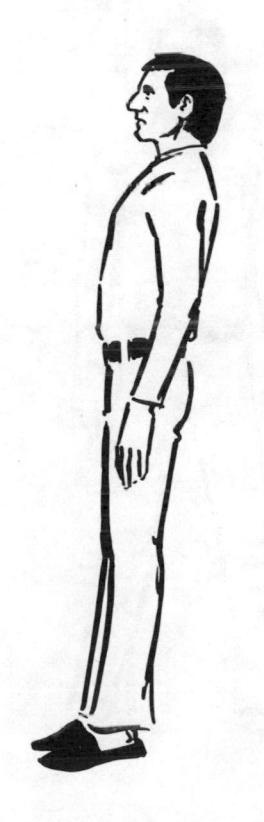

Forward Tilt   *Backward Tilt*

Double-zero position. Step open to the side, so that there are about fourteen inches of space between your heels. Now point to the left toe, and let it tilt the body over to the right, with the body in line with the left leg. Do not break at the hip. There will be a tendency to keep the upper body upright. Don't. Keep it in line, and keep the head in line. Then tilt back to the center. Now point the right toe, and let it tilt the body to the left. Do this back and forth many times, being sure to remain rigidly in line with the opposite leg. Now come back to the double-zero position and step forward about fourteen inches so that one foot is in front of the other and the weight is between them. Don't turn the feet out. Point the back toe, and let it push the body so that you are tilting forward, and looking toward the floor. Keep in line; don't break at the waist, head in line looking towards the floor. Back to the center. Now point the front toe, pushing the body back. Keep both knees straight on all of these tilts in all their directions. Do it several times, and then switch feet, and do it again. Stay rigid from the top of the head down.

42

Open Side Tilt

1.   2.

Open Tilts

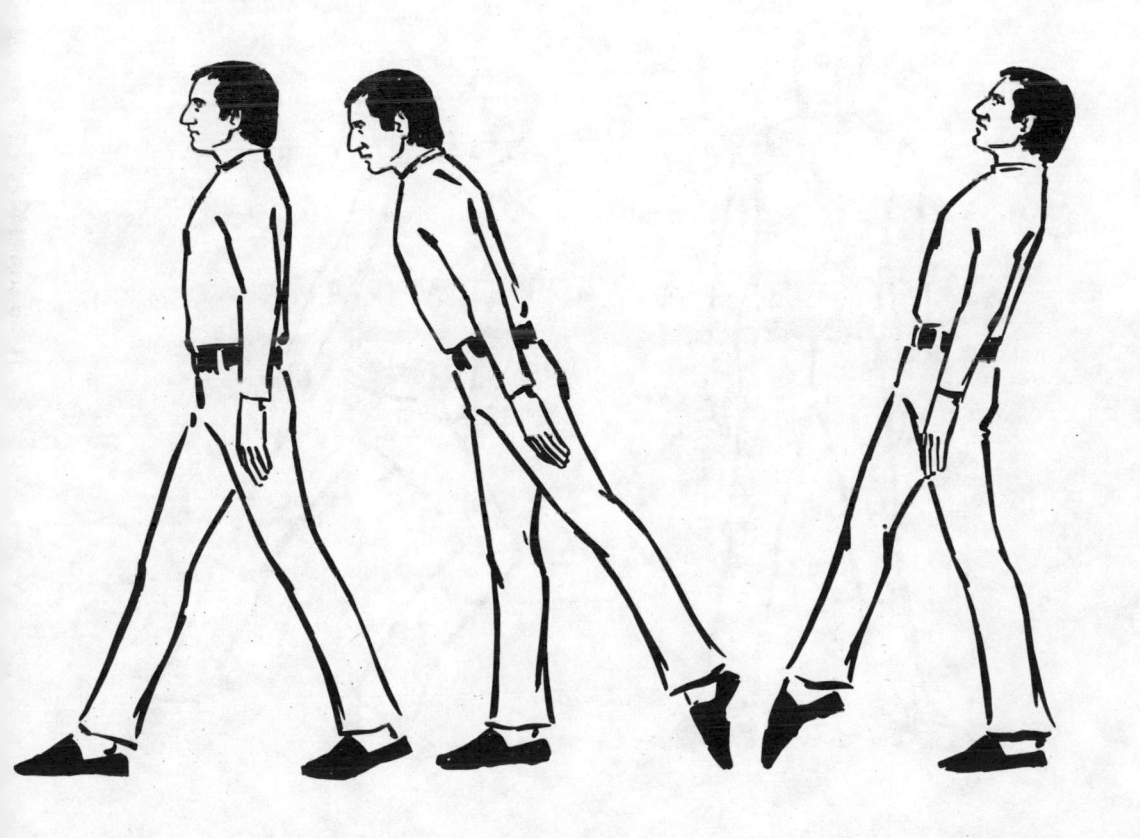

1. *Zero Position*   2. *Forward*   3. *Backward*

Unit Knee Bends: Double-zero position. Step open to the side, as you did for the tilts, but open your feet further. Stay upright, with the weight in the middle. Now, just bend the right knee. Do not break at the waist, and the body will tilt over to the right, on an angle that is in line with the left leg. Keep the head in line with the body. Do this over and over, and then on the left side. Now go back to the double-zero position, and step forward on the right foot, weight in the middle: a longer step than you did for the tilts. Don't turn the feet out. Now, bend the front knee, letting the body fall forward, and keeping it and the head in line with the back leg. Both heels stay on the floor. Up to the center. Do it many times, and then try bending the back knee, letting the body fall back a bit, everything in line with the front leg. Then, after doing this several times, alternate the forward and back ones. Now change feet, and go through it all again.

44

Unit Knee Bend to Side

1.

2.

Unit Knee Bend

1. *Backward*   2. *Forward*

Scale-Fulcrum Tilts: Double-zero position. Step open to the side. Tilt to the right, both legs straight, left toe pointed, body in line with the left leg, all the weight on the right. This is the starting position, and the finishing position. Put the arms along the body, one on each side of the left leg and keep them there. Now, using the body like a scale, with the right leg as the fulcrum, tilt over, lifting the left leg, and allowing the body to tilt over more. Then come back to the starting position. Then do it again, and go further. Keep both knees straight, and the body rigidly in line with the left leg. Only lift the left leg as far as the body goes over to the right; only go over with the body as far as the leg lifts. Don't try to go so far that the body breaks its line. Be sure the head stays in line with the body. When you get tired, try it on the other side.

47

1.

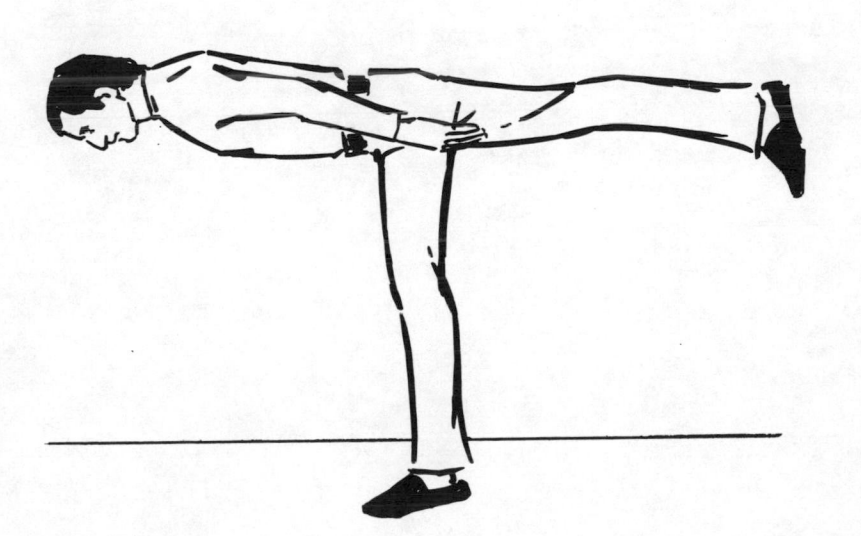

2.

Now go back to the double-zero position. Step forward on the right foot, weight between both. Point the left toe, tilting the body forward, body in line with the back leg, arms pointing back in line with the back leg. This is the starting and finishing position. Tilt the body over further, lifting the back leg, and keeping the body in line with it. Keep both knees straight. Back to the starting position. Do it many times, trying to tilt further, but not breaking the line of the body. When you get tired, try it with the other leg forward. Then do it to the rear, body tilted back, and in line with the front leg. You won't be able to tilt as far as to the rear. Tilt only as far as you can. Keep both knees straight on all of these. This next group starts in the same position: tilted to the right, body in line with the left leg, arms at the sides of the left leg, weight on the right. Now, as you tilt over, lifting the left leg, and tilting the body to the right, bend the right knee, and reach the left leg further to the left. You will be able to tilt much further over than you could when the right knee was straight. The further to the left you pull the left leg, and the deeper you bend the right knee, the further towards parallel you will get. Do this on the other side. Now use these movements to pick something up, like a basket, on each side. Now do it front and back. Step forward, tilt forward, and as you tilt forward, bend the standing knee, reaching the tilting leg back further, and keep the body in line. Use this movement to pick something up. Do it on the other side. Now to the rear. Tilt back. foot forward, and bend the back knee, reaching forward with the front leg as you go back. Now do it standing on the other leg. Try to keep the head in line with all of these: It will tend to remain upright, lifting as you go forward and dropping forward as you go back; don't let it.

49

1.

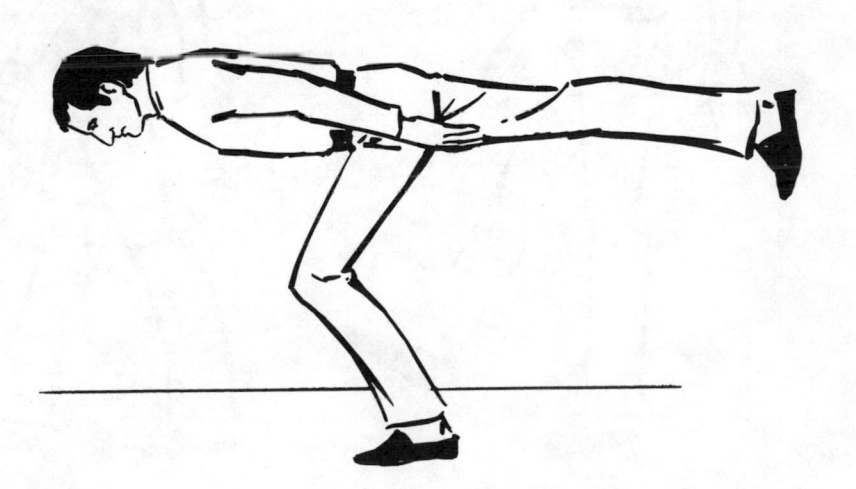

2.

All of these scale movements can be applied to moving or picking up objects. It gives a longer, more graceful line to the body, and provides clearer communication by being bigger. You can use them in your improvisations from now on, if you want them, and if they fit the character you are playing.

Sways: From the double-zero position tilt to the front, the side, and in all the directions of the compass. Now try to keep rigidly in line while you sway around in a circle. Now go the other way. Try to stay in line, and not to lead with your hips. Lead with your head.

Walks: The tin-soldier walk. Stand on your right foot with the left leg extended in front of you, with the foot flexed, and the body leaning back, in line with the raised leg. Both knees stay straight in this walk. Put the right arm forward and the left one back. As in walk #1, there are two moves: (1) step onto the left foot, putting all the weight on it, and bring the body upright. Do not move the arms on the step. (2) Change the leg and arms, so that the right leg is in the air in front, foot flexed, the body leaning back in line with it, the left arm is now forward and the right back. Continue. Be sure you do not move the arms on the step—only on the change. The body leans back, with the head in line with it when the foot is raised in front, and is upright when you step forward. You never really lean forward. Practice it very slowly, and when it is right, see how fast you can do the walk.

Walk With Body as a Unit

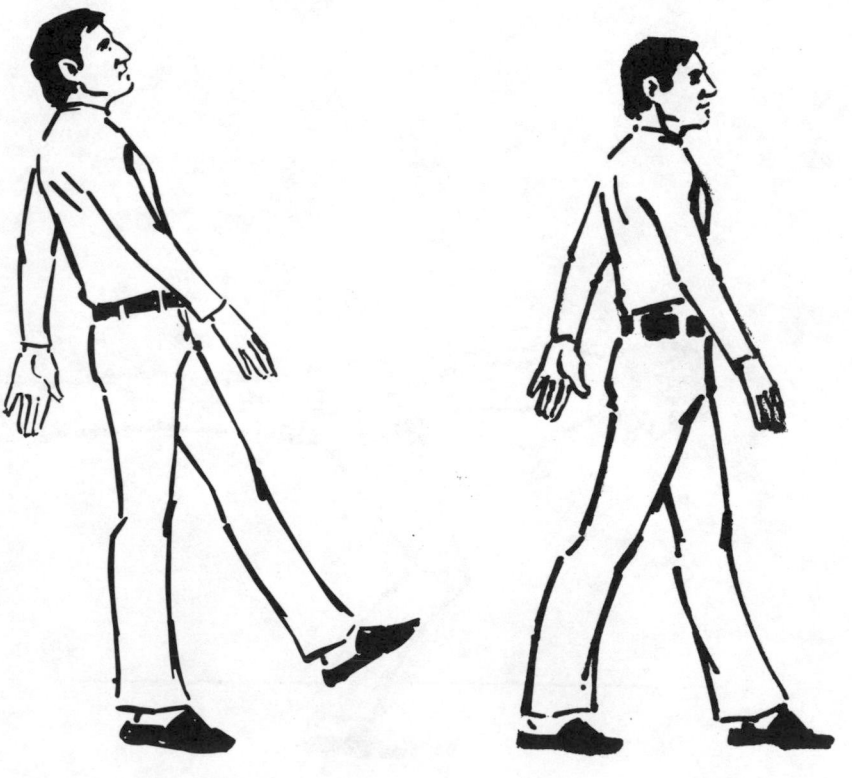

1.   2.

The stiff shuffle. Clasp your hands in front of you. Keeping the knees straight and the body rigid, shuffle the feet forward in tiny very quick sliding steps. When you do this walk, move in straight lines, and make square corners in your movement pattern. Be sure you keep your heels on the floor with this walk. The only time you would use either of these walks in a performance would be if the character you are portraying would walk in this very stylized manner—such as a wind-up toy.

Being Drunk: Drunkenness is based on the sway, and overcompensating for swaying too far. It is not based on a stagger. If you stagger, it is because you have swayed, overcompensated much too far, and so have lost your equilibrium. Sway, pull back as a recovery, and go too far in the opposite direction, which makes you pull back again. When you are drunk and walk towards someone, you are slightly off balance, so you don't aim right: You see you are going to miss them, so you sway towards them, but you go too far, so that now you will miss them in the other direction. Now, the real trick with all of this, is to try to appear sober while doing it. The drunk never tries to look drunk. He tries not to sway, tries to maintain his balance. The more you try not to show the sway and the lack of balance, the drunker you will look. Do it subtly.

51

Improvisations with the Body as a Unit: Handle objects, be some place, do some action, but don't break the line of the body. If you have to lean forward, let one leg go back; if you have to pick something up, do a tilt, etc.

Homework Assignment: Bring in a sketch in which the body is kept as a unit.

Inclination and rotation of each part separately; transtations; mirror exercise; transtation circles; illusion of climbing a ladder; duets.

Inclination and Rotation of Each Part Separately: Start in the double-zero position, and incline the head forward. Bring it back to the center. Repeat this several times. Now, keeping the same angle between the head and neck, incline just the neck forward, and bring it back up. You will feel it pull at the back of the neck. Do this several times. Don't let the head incline too far—keep it in line with the neck. Now incline the head forward, keep it there, and incline the neck forward: bring the neck up, and then the head. Now the chest: Incline it forward while keeping the head and neck in line with it, and then back to center, and do it several times. Then incline the head, then the neck, and then the chest forward, and then up in the usual manner: chest, then neck, then head. Now incline just the waist forward, keeping the head, neck and chest in line with it. Keep the pelvis tucked under. This should be like a little bow. Do it several times until you can really feel where the waist is. Then incline the head, neck, chest, and waist, forward, and come up one piece at a time. Now incline just the pelvis forward, breaking at the top of the leg, and letting the pelvis go back a bit, like a big bow. Now incline forward in the usual manner, one piece at a time, and then come up.

52

1. *Double-Zero Position*

2. *Head*

3. *Neck*

4. *Chest*

5. *Waist*

6. *Pelvis*

Now to the side: Incline the head to the right, center, and then to the left, then center, and keep alternating. Then incline the neck to the right, keeping the head in line with it: It feels like a transtation of the head, but the head stays in line with the neck. Then back to center, and then to the left, and center. Now incline the head to the right, and the neck, and now, having done the neck alone, you should be better able to feel how to pull the neck up to the center, and then the head. Do it on both sides. Now incline the chest to the right, keeping the head and neck in line with it, like the top half of a marionette, and back to center and then on the other side, several times. Now incline the head, then neck, then chest to the right, and then up, and then to the left and up. Now the waist: The inclination of the waist alone will feel like a transtation of the chest, except that the head, neck and chest should stay in line with the waist instead of breaking. Pull the waist back to the center, letting it pull the pieces that are attached to it back to the center. Do it on the other side. Keep alternating, trying most of all to feel the waist lifting to the center by itself. Now incline the head, then neck, then chest, then waist to the right, and then up one at a time, and then to the left. Now the pelvis: Incline it to the right, keeping the rest of the body in line with it, so that you tilt, with the left knee bending, and the left foot going to the half-toe. Now back to the center, then the other side, and then do the entire side inclination to each side.

Side Tilt

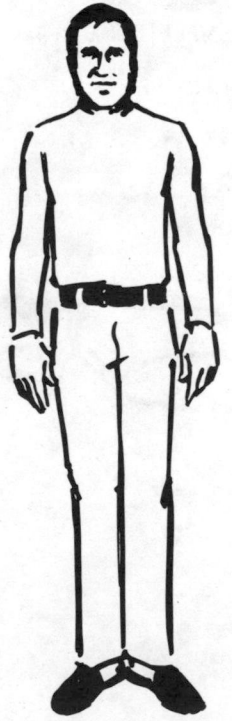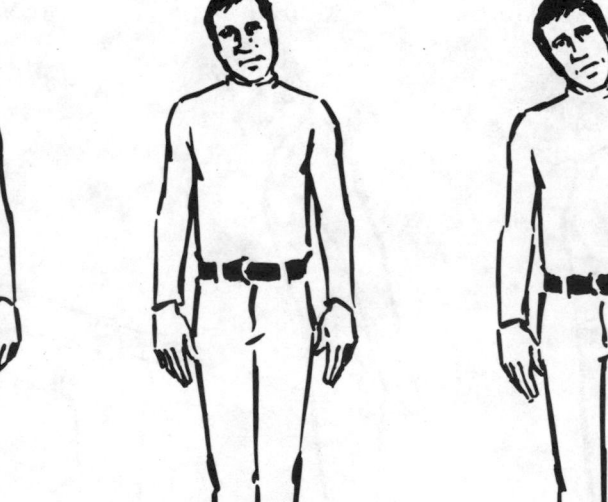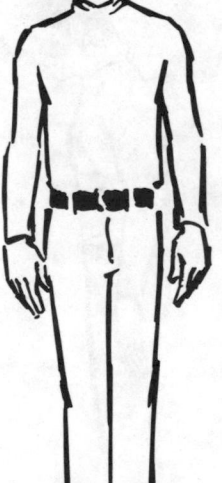

1. *Double-Zero Position*   2. *Head*   3. *Neck*

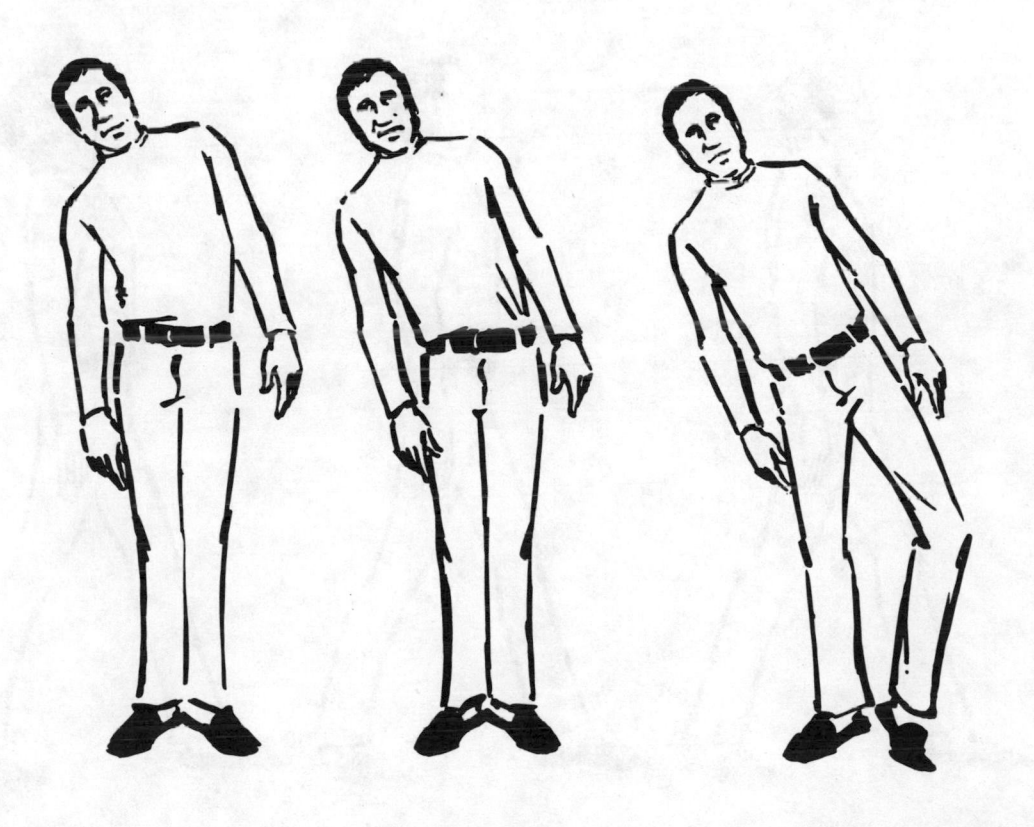

4. Chest   5. Waist   6. Pelvis

Do the same principle to the rear, one piece at a time.

Inclination to Rear

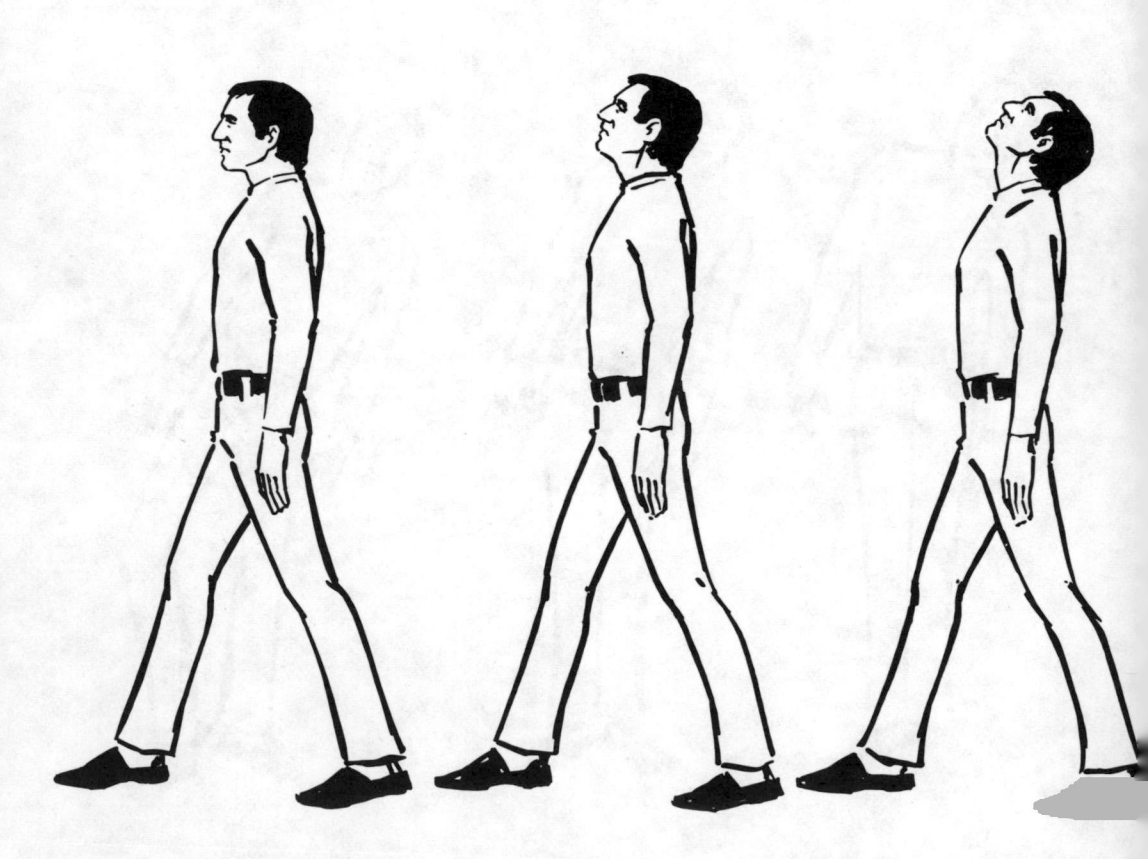

1. Double-Zero Position   *2. Head*   *3. Neck*

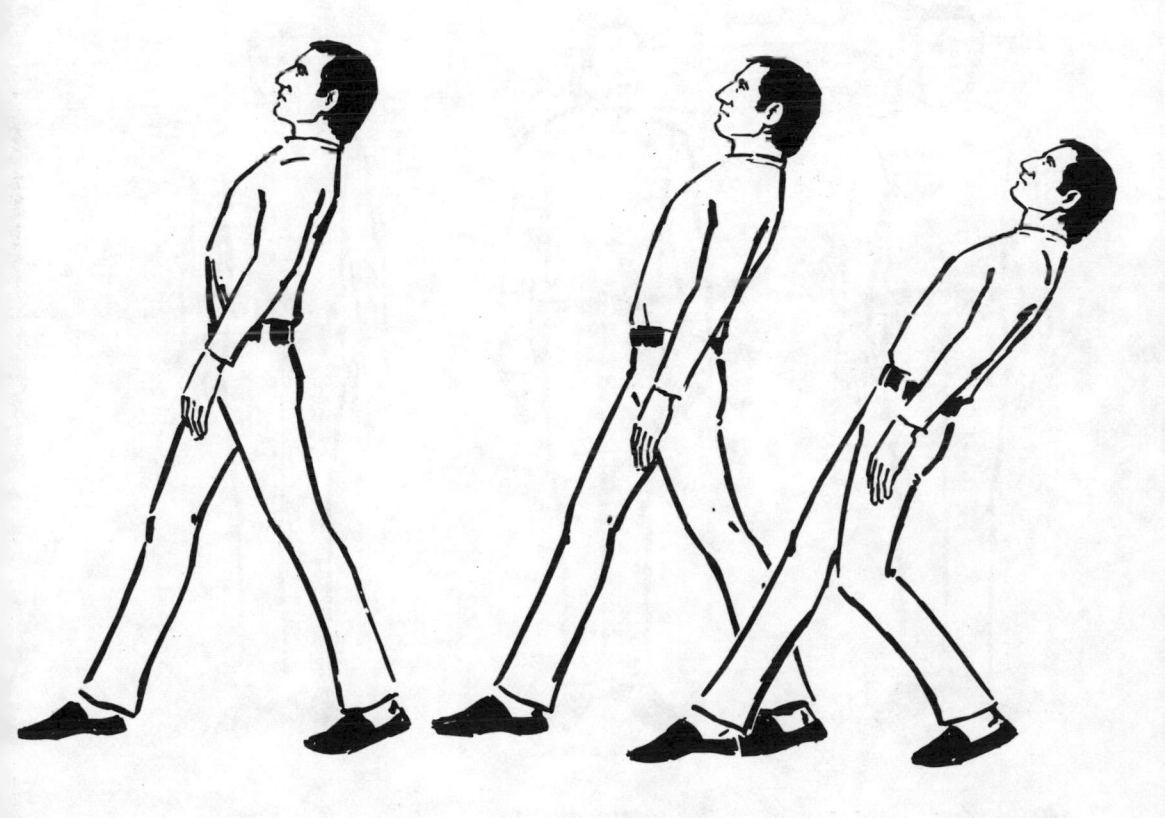

4. *Chest*　　　　5. *Waist*　　　　6. *Pelvis*

For the rotation, the difficult parts will be the neck and the waist. When you do the waist, try to hold the pelvis locked in place, and to twist just the waist around and back.

By the time you finish this sequence, you should be all stretched apart, but you should understand the inclinations and rotations better.

Do the transtations.

58

Rotation

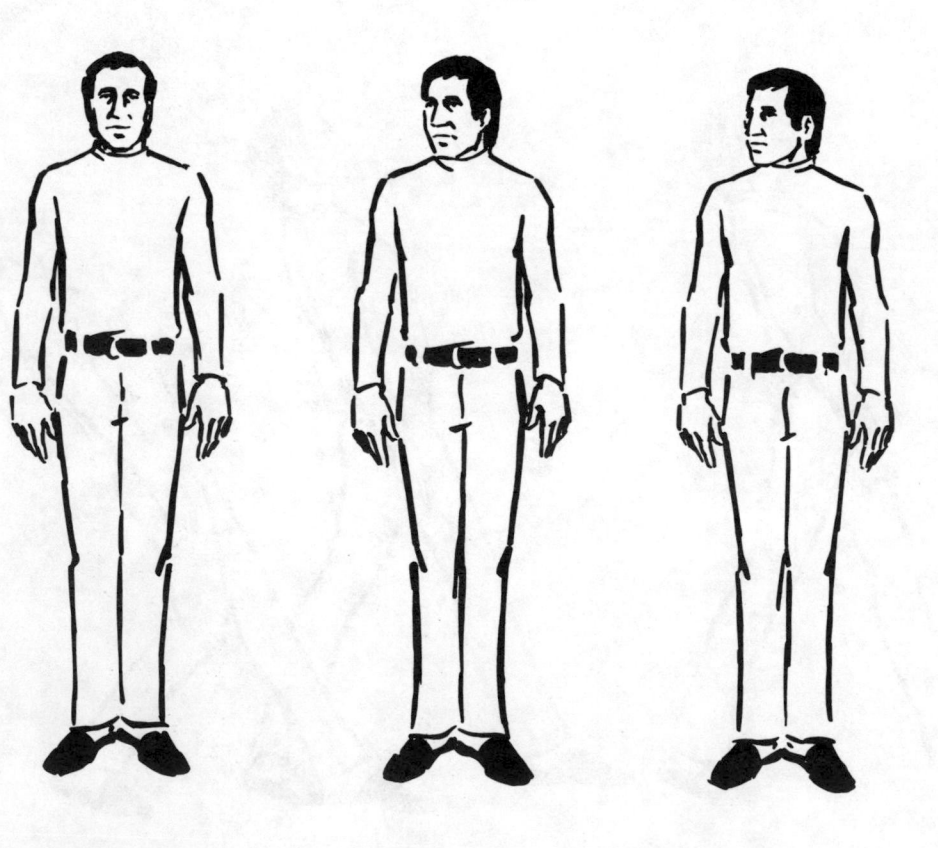

1. *Double-Zero Position*   2. *Head*   3. *Neck*

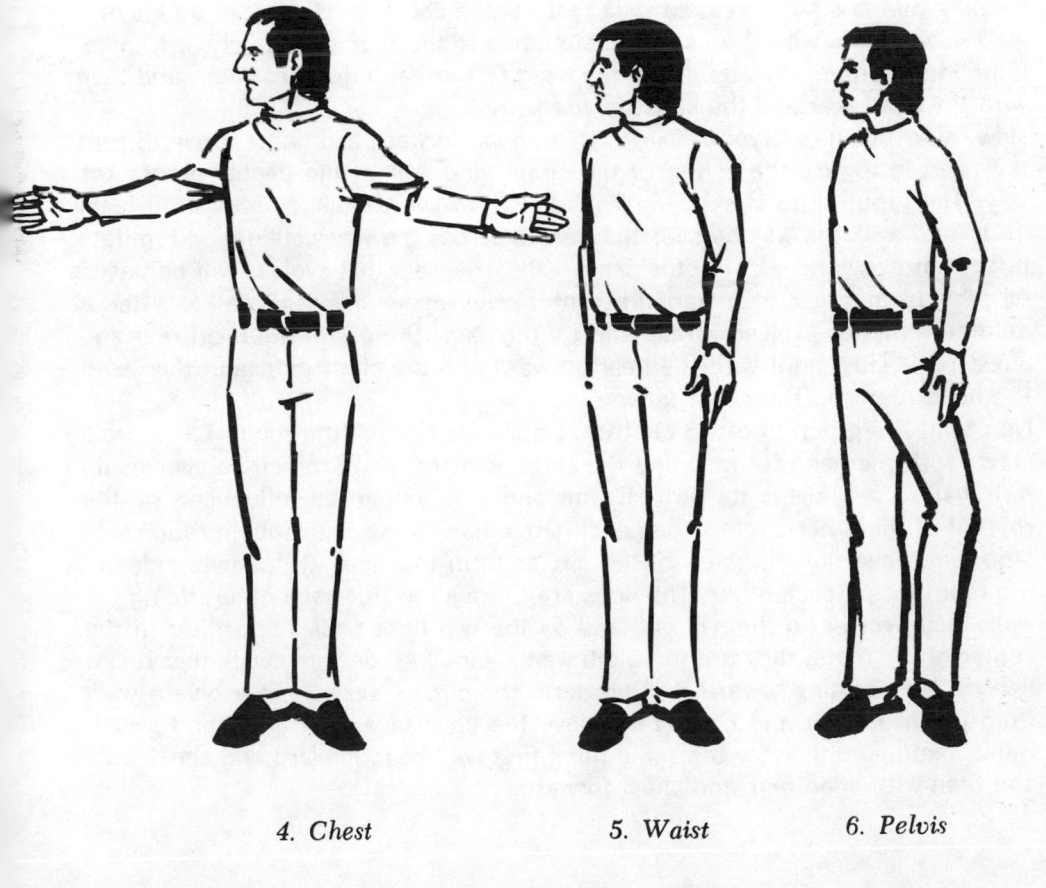

4. Chest   5. Waist   6. Pelvis

Mirror Exercise: Have the group divide into partners, with each partner facing the other, about three feet away. Person "A" of each duet is to do an action, such as putting on theatrical makeup, or making a salad, etc., and the other one, person "B," is to mirror the action: Do exactly the same motions at the same moment. Person "A" is to try to help "B" to follow, by moving fairly slowly, and by, in a subtle way, following at the same time that he is leading. Person "B" can follow best if he looks towards the eyes of person "A": He will be able to see both hands with peripheral vision; if he watches one hand, he may lose the other one. If "A" uses his right hand, "B" is to use his left—a mirror image. They begin, and do this for a while, until the instructor calls "switch," at which point "B" leads, and "A" follows. When "B" starts to lead, he is to continue the same action and rhythm that they were in while "A" was leading. It can change, but it should be gradual. When "switch" is called again, "A" leads again. The time between calls of "switch" should become shorter and shorter, and finally, the instructor should call "Both follow." At this point, they continue the action, both trying to follow, neither leading. This is the essence of the game: Neither ego should be in the forefront; both should be surrendered to the activity.

Transtation Circles: Have everyone make a circle around the room, facing counter-clockwise. All transtation the head forward, and the chest forward, and keeping that position, create a walk that fits the character. Each can do his own walk. Then try it with the head transtationed to the rear and the chest transtationed to the rear. Then do it with the head forward and the chest rear, and then with the head rear and the chest forward.

Now, start again, everyone is in a circle, head forward and chest forward; turn the head in toward the center of the circle, and look at the people across the way. The group is to start to walk, and is to evolve a walk: No one is to lead, each is to walk the way he sees the people across the way walking, and imitate it, so that everyone is doing the same walk. The walk that evolves will be based on who is in the circle, and different circles make different walks. After a definite walk has evolved, break and try the same thing with the head rear and chest rear. Then do it with the head forward and the chest rear, and then with the head rear and the chest forward.

Now split the group into two circles, at opposite ends of the room. Each circle starts with the head forward and the chest forward, and each circle evolves its own walk: Each keeps its own rhythm and tries not to be influenced by the rhythm of the other circle. When each circle has its own individual group walk, stop, and have the members of the circles form two lines at opposite sides of the room facing each other. The lines are to walk towards each other, doing the walk they evolved in their circle, and as the two lines pass each other in the center of the room, they are to switch walks. Line "A" does the walk that it saw line "B" do coming toward it. Then form the circles again, and evolve a walk from the head rear and chest rear, have the lines face each other and switch walks again, and then try the same thing first with head forward and chest rear, and then with head rear and chest forward.

Illusion of Climbing a Ladder: Imagine a ladder in front of you. Place your hands on two of the rungs, one higher than the other: right higher, and left on the lower rung. Keeping the right hand still, let the left hand release its rung, and place it on the rung that is next higher than the one the right is on. Stop. There should be about ten inches between rungs. Now, keeping the relationship between the two hands, keeping ten inches between them, move them both downward about ten inches, so that now the left is at the level the right was on, and the right is down where the left was in the starting position. Stop. Now release the rung with the right hand, and place the right on the rung that is higher than the one the left is now on. Stop. Now move them both downward ten inches, keeping the space between them. You always maintain the distance between these imaginary rungs. Keep doing this over and over until it is familiar. As you release the hand from the lower rung and place it on the higher one, say to yourself the words, "Round, place," and as you move both hands downward the ten inches, say to yourself, "Climb."

61

Climbing a Ladder

1.   2.

The feet: Lift your right foot into the air, as if you were going to put it on the next rung of a ladder, but since there is no ladder there, place the half-toe of the foot on the floor, next to the left foot—the right knee is now bent. As you do this, say to yourself, "Round, place." Next, rise up on the half-toe of both feet, straightening both knees, so you're way up, and when you've reached the top, come down, bending the left knee, and going to the half-toe of the left foot. As you do this, say to yourself, "Climb." Now lift the left foot from the half-toe in a climbing movement, and then put it back on the half-toe, then rise up again, and then bend the right again. Keep doing this over and over until it's familiar. The words for the hands and the legs are the same, and they coordinate that way.

3.

4.

Start with the right knee bent, and the left hand low. On "Round, place," at the same time, place the left hand on the higher rung as you lift the right foot in its climbing motion and put it back down on its half-toe. On "Climb," rise up on both toes, straightening both knees, as you pull both hands down the ten inches. Keep going. It gets easier every day you practice it.

Next, look at the homework assignment.

Now, if there's time, do some duets.

Homework Assignment: Chest impulses with handling objects.

LESSON SEVEN

Inclinations; rotations; chest impulses; pelvic impulses; illusions of pushing and pulling; climbing; illusory walk #1; duets.

Do the inclinations, rotations, and chest impulses.
Look at the homework assignment.

Pelvic Impulses: Whenever possible, the impulse for the action should come from the pelvis, flow through the chest, and then reach the extremities. It makes the action even bigger and clearer than just the chest impulse.

Point the right toe to the side, knee straight. As you shift the weight to the right leg, put the heel down, and lead with the pelvis, then feel the flow up through the chest, allow the chest to lift the arm up as if it were going to pick an apple. All the weight is now on the right leg, and the arm is up in the air, both knees straight, the left toe pointed or on the half-toe. To come back: Put the left heel down, lead with the pelvis towards the left, then let it flow through the chest, which inclines to the right, pulling the arm down. Do it a few times on each side. Now do the same thing forward and back, shifting the weight forward, and flowing through the chest into the arms, and leading with the pelvis to come back.

Now point the right toe forward. We are going to pick something up off the floor. Step forward onto the right, leading with the pelvis, lift the chest which lifts the arm, and as the arm comes up, bend the right knee, extending the left leg back, as we did in the body as a unit. Keep the body in line with the left leg; pick up the object. Now, to come up, the first move is to tuck the pelvis under, hard, breaking the line of the body, and allow the momentum from this to lift your body. Do not start up until the pelvis has hit its final position in tucking under, and let this carry you. The body breaks in this: Don't keep the body as a unit on the way up. Try this on the other side. You can use either hand with either leg forward. From now on, whenever you pick something up, tuck under a bit, and let the impulse from the pelvis lead you.

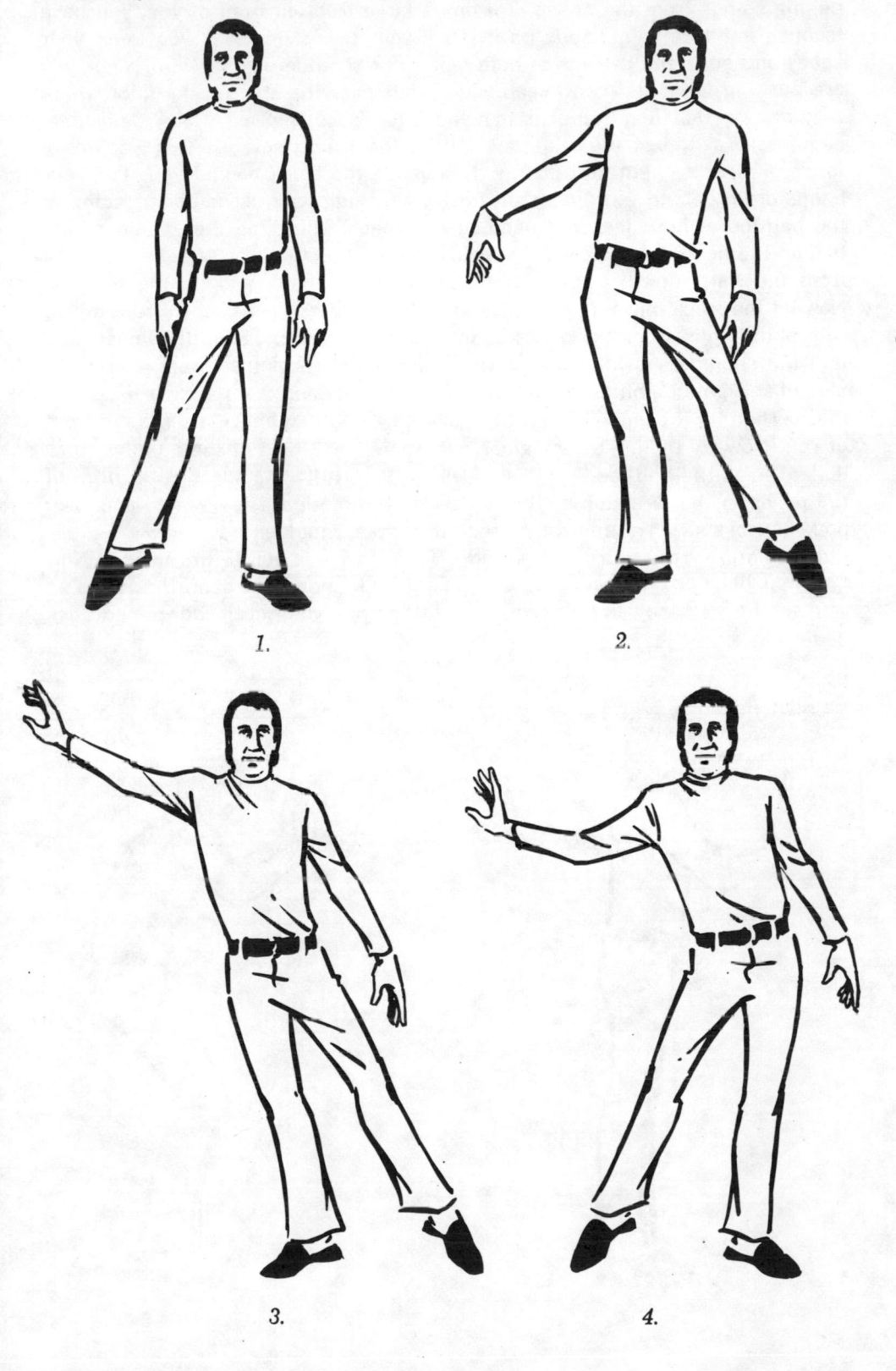

1.

2.

3.

4.

Illusions of Pushing and Pulling: The impulse for all illusions of pushing and pulling comes from the pelvis. Imagine a large truck in front of you; you have to push it. Place your hands on it. Tuck your pelvis under as you bend your knees and go to the half-toe of both feet. Your shoulders go forward, since you are pushing forward. Try to keep your hands over the spot on the floor where they are, so that it will appear that the truck is not moving. Relax, and do it again several times, the last time letting the truck move so that you move forward. Use strength and energy. Now place the truck behind you. Put your hands down behind you against it. Push by tucking your pelvis under, going to the half-toe of both feet and bending the knees. This time the shoulders are behind the pelvis because you are going in that direction. It is exactly the same from the waist down: pelvis tucked under, knees bent, and on the half-toe. Now let the truck move. Now take hold of a stuck dresser drawer in front of you with both hands. Tuck the pelvis under, go to the half-toe, bend the knees, and pull the shoulders behind the pelvis in the direction of the thrust. The arms should straighten a bit as you do this to give the illusion that the drawer doesn't move. Then let it come out. Try this same move with an imaginary rope in front of you. Now try pulling an imaginary rickshaw. Take hold of the handles, tuck under, go to the half-toe with the knees bent, and the shoulders go in front of the pelvis in the direction of the thrust. Do the motion a few times, and then pull the rickshaw. Try this with a rope over your shoulder.

Apply this principle to a stuck window: Tuck under as you try to open it. Now lift a bar bell with the same principle: First tuck under and bend the knees as you go the half-toe, and then as you lift it, put your heels down and tuck under more.

66

Pushing

1.

2.

Pushing (Rear)

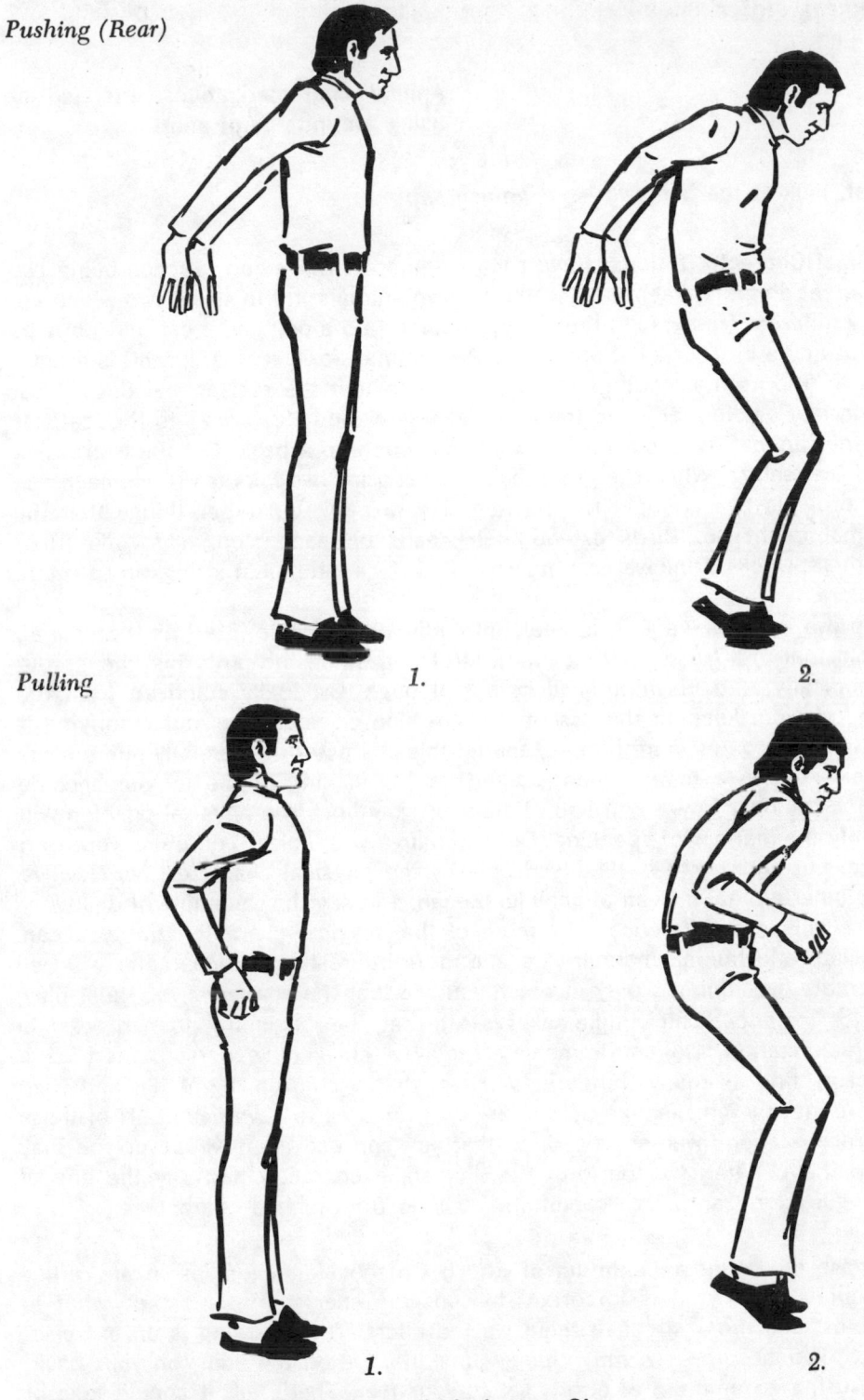

Pulling

1.

2.

67

1.

2.

Practice climbing a ladder, as we did in Lesson Six.
Practice the illusory walk, as we did in Lesson Four.
Do an improvisation using the pelvic impulses in the course of your story.
Homework Assignment: Bring in a sketch using pelvic impulses.

Animal characterizations; exercise on using a minimum of effort.

First, look at the homework assignments.

Animal Characterizations: Have each member of the group practice being two different animals. Each is to select his own animals; try to select two which are very different from each other. They shouldn't do a dog and a cat, but perhaps a dog and a bird, or a cat and a fish. Any animal, fowl, reptile, insect, is alright. Try to find as many things to do as you can that the real animal does. Most important are the face and the attitude. Stretch your features into the features of your animal: If it is a bird, extend your lips into a beak. Get the expression and the feeling. When the group has practiced for five minutes or so, each can perform his two animals for the rest. Try to point out other things that the animal might do. Birds extend their heads on each step, and ruffle their feathers. Ducks drink water. Cats wash their face, and hit at string, and stretch. Explore.

Step two is to evolve your animals into animallike people. Start as the animal, for instance, a frog; the frog has a stretched smile, he puffs his cheeks out periodically, and his tongue flicks out at bugs. Gradually stand up from the frog position, keeping the essential expression on your face, but modifying it so that it becomes more human, and let this character occasionally puff out his cheeks, but in a human manner, and let his flicking of the tongue become licking the lips. Now say a line of dialogue, any line. The physical position will modify the manner of speaking. Do not change your voice: Try to use your own voice, but allow it to be changed only by the physical character. Now evolve your other animal into an animallike human, and say the same line of dialogue. There will be a difference. The more of the physical characteristics you can translate into human mannerisms, the more interesting the character will be. If you are ever doing a play in which you see that the character you must play is, for instance, chickenlike, always start at the beginning to achieve your characterization. Do not immediately play a chickenlike person; start as a chicken, find as many things as you can that a chicken might do, and then evolve into the chickenlike person. It is a good idea to have five or six of these characterizations well-practiced, so that you can use them whenever you may need them. When you perform the animallike character and say the line of dialogue, don't show the evolution—just do the finished characters.

Exercise on Using a Minimum of Effort: On the stage, just as in any other strenuous activity, it is important to conserve energy. You must do what is simplest and most direct, without wasted effort. The following is an exercise, which, if done properly, may change your life. Lie on the floor, on your back, and, using a minimum of effort, get to your feet. That's all. It should take at least five minutes. Feel as if you have been going through the desert for three day, without food or water, and you have no strength or energy left. You must use leverage to get to your feet: Don't lift anything when you can slide it, try staying limp; use one part of your body to move another. Gradually find your way to your feet, and don't stop until you are all the way up. If you do it right, it will make you high. It will give you the experience of using a minimum of effort, and that experience can stay with you and influence your future performances. It is even better if you take ten or fifteen minutes.

Homework Assignment: Bring in a sketch using a character based on an animal in a short scene.

Inclinations; rotations; transtations; tug-of-war; hand exercises; illusory walks #1 and #2; walks with a high knee; takes; improvisation with sneak and take.

Do the inclinations, rotations, chest impulses, and transtations.
Practice the tug-of-war and the hand exercises. Do the first illusory walk as we practiced it in Lesson Four.

70   **Illusory Walk #2:** This is another walk in place that looks like you're actually covering ground while you remain in place. It works on a different principle from the first illusory walk; the arms are easier with this one, but the legs are more difficult. Starting position: place your right foot on its half-toe, with the raised heel pointing towards your left ankle, and place your left arm forward, so that it is in opposition to the bent right knee. Your right foot should be close enough to the left one so that if you lower the heel it will almost touch the left instep. There are 2 halfs to practice in this walk: Lean your weight onto the right half-toe; as you press the right heel to the floor, lift the left leg (with the knee remaining straight) to the rear, so that it is about 12 inches off the floor. The right knee should become straight as the right heel touches the floor. The arms do not move at all. Stop. Then pull the left leg back into its former position on the floor as you bend the right knee, and rock back up onto the half-toe of the right foot. You are now in the starting position again. Keep doing this over and over, without moving the arms. Try it on the other side many times. Now all you need is the change between. From the beginning: You are on the half-toe of the right, with the right knee bent, and the heel towards the left instep; shift the weight onto the right half-toe, then press the right heel down, lifting the left leg to the rear. Be sure at this point that both knees are straight. Now change the leg and arms: Place the left foot on its half-toe, near the right foot, with the left knee bent, and the heel pointing towards the right instep. Change the arms with the change of legs, so that the right arm is now forward. Shift the weight onto the left half-toe, press the left heel down, lifting the right leg behind you. Both knees are now straight, left heel on the floor. Change the leg and arms, shift the weight, and continue. It is important to straighten the knee of the leg whose heel is pressing toward the floor, and it is most important not to change the arms except while the leg is changing. The shoulders may change with the arms, to give a twist to the body, but the body from the pelvis down should remain straight flat forward, without rotating at all, and without the knees turning in. The legs should be turned out for this walk.

This walk is the basis of the illusion of walking against the wind (practice it until it is smooth, and then imagine a gust of wind blowing at you, and let the body adjust) and of ice-skating.

Illusory Walk #2

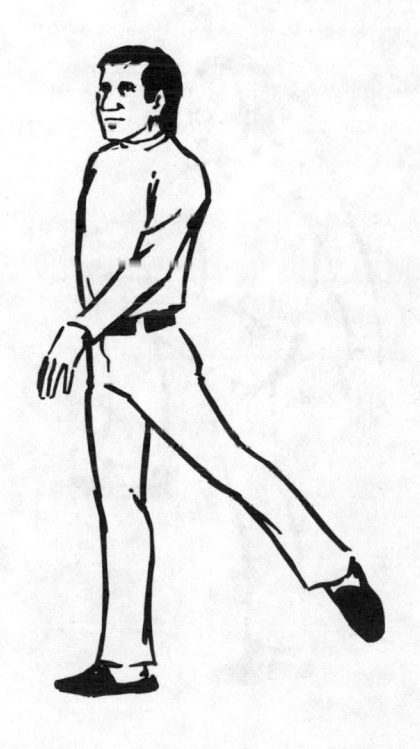

1.   2.

Walk with a High Knee: There are four walks with a high knee, but we will only do one now. These are sneaky walks, and are classic in form. Stand straight: 1. Lift the right knee as high as you can, foot flexed, and put the left arm forward, and the right arm back. The left knee remains straight; the balance should be vertical, and the right heel should be pulled as far back and in as it can, with the knee pulling up. 2. Bend the left knee, lifting the right knee higher, and keeping the foot flexed with the heel in. The body should remain vertical; don't lean back, and keep the left arm forward. 3. Extend the right leg and foot forward, keeping the foot flexed, and reach a bit further forward with the left hand. Don't move anything else. 4. When the right leg is extended as far as it will go, even if the knee is not straight, point the right toe. 5. Continue the pointing motion, and bring the foot down until it touches the floor. The left knee is still bent, and the weight is still on the left foot, with the left arm reaching forward. 6. Shift the weight forward onto the right foot, sliding through, allowing the right knee to bend, but keeping the left arm reaching forward, until all the weight is on the right. Then change: Lift the left foot up off the floor, knee high, straighten up, straighten the right leg, left heel in and foot flexed, and right arm forward. You are now in position #1, again on the other side. Be sure you regain your balance on #1, and are really up straight. Do the walk from this side, and continue. It takes a while to become smooth, and it generally stays slow. Each move can flow into the next one, but be sure you complete each one.

High Knee Walk #1

1.   2.

73

3.    4.

5.    6.

Takes: A take is a look. They are a comedic and/or dramatic device that should be practiced physically, but won't work unless they are motivated in performance. The denomination of the take tells you the number of turns of the head —a double take is two turns, triple take is three turns, etc. There must always be an emotional reaction on a take. There are two ways to do the single or simple take: you are walking, and something catches your attention out of the corner of your eye; you stop, turning your head at the same time towards what you see. The second way is to stop first, wait a moment, and **then** snap your head towards the event or object. There is only one turn of the head. For the **double take,** there is a prelude, and then it is the same. You are walking along, your head drifts around to the side, and drifts back as you keep going; suddenly you stop and snap your head around because something has registered. The first turn of the head must have no reaction: It is nonchalant. The reaction takes place after you've brought your head back. The second way to do the double take is like the second single take: You walk, your head drifts around, it drifts back, you walk on, suddenly you stop, wait, and **then** snap your head towards what you have seen. One way is to stop and turn at the same time; the other way is to stop, wait, and then turn. The triple take, or quadruple or more are the same, except that each time you turn the head your reaction must be bigger. You can go on until you cannot get a bigger expression and reaction. The slow take is the same, except that for the last turn of the head, you do it very slowly, as if you cannot believe what you have seen.

You should practice takes both to the right and to the left, moving and in place, big and small.

If there is time, do an improvisation which starts by sneaking on, and which has a take in it.

Look at the homework assignment.

Homework Assignment: Diminution of the action. Bring in a short exercise within which an object is handled, using slow and clear chest impulses for all the arm movements. Do it very slowly, with exaggerated chest impulses. Then do the same exercise again, this time smoothing out the action, rounding the corners, and giving only a suggestion of the chest impulses. Do it this time at a normal speed. If you practice the slow version enough times, the faster version is easy.

Falls; stage trips; fainting; the illusory run; sitting; climbing a ladder; illusory walks #1 and #2; improvisations with falls.

The purpose of learning falls is so that you can get to the ground without hurting yourself. The technique only gets you to the ground; after that you must be an actor, and forget technique. There are three series of falls.

75

The Rigid Falls: Stand on your knees, toes pointed back, pelvis tucked under tightly, arms hanging at your sides. Keep pressing the toes to the floor, and fall forward. As you fall forward, you must do two things: breathe out (so that if you hit hard there will be no air to bump against your diaphragm) and turn your head to the side (so you won't bump your chin). Your arms will automatically come forward to catch you. You do not have to put your hands forward, they will do it instinctively. So don't worry about catching yourself: If you didn't have the instinct to catch yourself, you would not have survived to adulthood, so have faith that your hands will catch you. Do not break at the pelvis. Try this a few times. Between falls, do not wait on your knees; never stay on your knees more than a minute or two: It can do permanent damage to the cartilage in the knee, unless you condition it very slowly over a long period of time. (Don't let a director make you stay on your knees for a ten minute scene—tell him I said you're not allowed to).
Stand up. The straight forward fall is the same principle as the one on the knees. As you fall straight forward, without breaking the body, breathe out, and turn your head to the side. Once again your arms will catch you. Only do this one a couple of times. Those who lack courage can try it on a rug, on grass, or at the beach. Don't do it on a bed—too springy.
I'm afraid you'll have to see me personally for the straight back fall (or see George Hopkins, the comedian, who taught it to me).

The Moving Falls: In this series you step in the direction of the fall. So that if you are to fall forward, you would step forward onto the right foot, bending the right knee deeply, put your hands on the floor, and then lower your body. The knee can turn in or out. Then do it with the left leg stepping forward. The hands always hit the floor before the body. Do the same principle to the side: If you are to fall to the right, step to the right, bending the right knee deeply, put the hands on the floor in the direction you are falling, and then your body hits. The same thing to the left. And then the rear. When you fall backwards you step back, bending a bit forward, your hands catch you, and then your body hits. These falls are impact falls: You have been hit, or bumped; there has been a blow or a bullet, and the impact carries you in the direction it was going. They're used in all fight scenes.

The In-place Falls: The principle behind this series is the fulcrum. You basically remain in place, and one leg moves in the opposite direction of the fall. If you are to fall forward, bend the right knee, extending the left leg backwards, put the hands on the floor in front of you, and then the body hits. If you are falling right, bend the right knee, extend the left leg to the left, so that your weight remains in the same place, put your hands on the floor under your right side, and continue to the ground. Same to the left. This side in-place fall is the basis of fainting on the stage. Do it limply, and you will see it. You can do it without hands by bending the upper torso in the opposite direction as you fall: but be sure to keep extending the leg in the direction opposite the fall for balance. When you do this to the rear, extend the foot forward, hands under you, and land. This one is the basis for the famous banana peel fall.

76

Stage Trips: To trip, just walk, and during one step, as one foot passes the other, catch the toe of the moving foot behind the heel of the foot that is on the floor, and then continue the step. If the impact of the toe hitting the heel also bends the knee of the in-place foot, it will be a more violent trip. React as if you have tripped over something. When you do this, be sure you don't anticipate it. Be surprised when it happens (or angry) (or **some**thing).

The Illusory Run: This looks like you are running, but you remain in place. Crouch forward. Stand on your left foot, left knee bent, right leg extended in the air in front of you, body forward, and both arms on the right side of your body, extended back. The right knee in the air is bent, the foot is flexed, but relaxed. Swing the right leg way back, brushing the toe on the floor in passage, and at the same time swing both arms forward. Swing the leg forward and the arms back. Do this several times. When it swings free and easy, do it with a jump—the standing leg leaving the floor as the swinging one passes it, and landing back on the floor as the swinging one reaches its final position forward, or final position back. Jump on each pass. You may look back with the leg as it goes back every few times if you are supposed to be followed by a pursuer. Try it on the other side. The downstage foot is the one that should swing, so you should be proficient with both legs—there's no telling in which direction you'll have to run.

1.

2.

Sitting: When you have to sit in mime, without a chair, don't try to sit low; just give a suggestion of sitting. Put one foot forward a bit, and throw one hip back as you sit, so your weight is on the back foot, and your back is up straight. When you get tired, pull the front foot in, shift the weight to the other hip, and put the other foot forward. You can maintain your balance while crossing your leg or putting your foot on your knee, if you maintain a secure base.

Practice climbing a ladder.

Practice illusory walks #1 and #2.

Have each one do an improvisation which includes a fall.

Look at the homework.

Homework Assignment: If your school is on the quarter system, this will be the last class of the quarter, and the next thing brought in will be the final, which should be a three to five minute sketch, with a beginning, a middle and an end, which uses whatever technique is needed to tell the story. It should be well rehearsed, and well performed.

If you are on the semester, or some other system, and there are continuing classes, the assignment should be to bring in a sketch which includes a fall.

Inclination and rotation of each part separately; beginning and advanced hand exercises; walks #1 and #2, duets.

First run through the inclinations and rotations, and then do each part separately as in Lesson Six.

Do the hand exercises we have done.

Advanced Hand Exercises

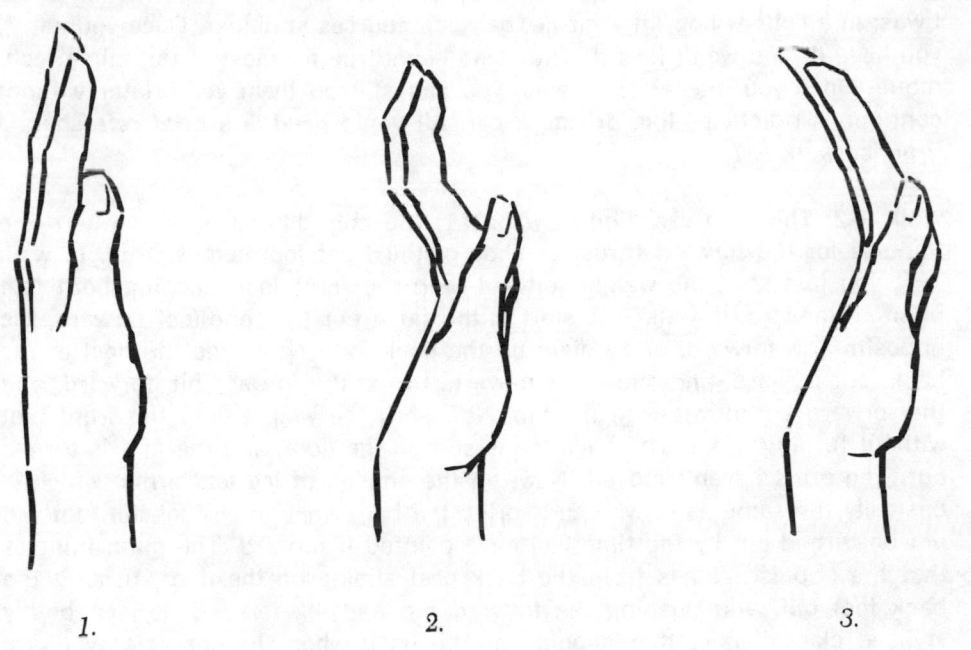

1.   2.   3.

Advanced Hand Exercises: This exercise is designed to give great flexibility and snakelike suppleness to your hands, but it takes many months to perfect, so don't be impatient. Hold both hands in front of you, fingers up, elbows down, thumbs toward you. The hands should be relaxed, with the fingers extended, and almost touching. The elbows must stay down and not move during this. Move #1 is to press the lowest knuckles in towards each other, while keeping the fingers gently curved. The left hand will now look like an elongated "S," and the right will be its opposite. Practice this over and over: pressing the knuckles in, and relaxing them. Move #2 is to practice keeping your hands stiff and straight, facing each other, with the fingers bent back as far as possible, and, being sure not to bend the lowest knuckles at all, bend the wrists forward as far as they can go. They will not go far, if you keep all knuckles straight. Practice this over and over; be sure your elbows stay down: Only the wrist moves. Now to combine them: Start with the hands upright, facing each other, elbows down, fingers extended and relaxed. (1) Push the lowest knuckles towards each other. (2) Keep the pushed-in position of the knuckles, and at the same time bend the wrists in so that the hands move towards each other, and gradually straighten the other fingers so that they are in line with the bent-back lowest knuckles. Only go as far as you can go without bending the lowest knuckles. (3) You are now in the same position you were when we practiced #2 above. Now relax the whole hand back into its starting position, letting the relaxation start at the wrist, and flow, curving up through the lowest knuckles, the higher ones, and finally up through the finger-tips. That's it: Practice it every day for a few minutes, and in a couple of months you may have it.

80 When I first met Marcel Marceau in 1955, and he saw my group perform and invited me to come to Paris to work with him, I asked him what I should practice. He did the above hand-wriggle, and said "This." When I saw him seven months later, I had it. I practiced it all the time until I got it, anywhere I was: in a coffee shop, in a movie, between courses at dinner. Once you get it, you have it, and won't lose it. The same holds true for most of the mime technique. Once you master the walks, you can still do them years later without continuous practice—like driving a car: All you'd need is a brief refresher. Practice walk #1.

Walk #2: This is a variation of walk #1; the only difference is in where the impulse for the forward thrust or slide of the front foot comes from. In walk #1, you just shift the weight forward onto the front foot, keeping both feet pointing forward. In walk #2, start in the same position: one foot forward, the opposite arm forward, and weight on the back foot. Now slide the heel of the back foot forward, and allow this move to thrust the forward hip forward, and the forward leg moves with the hip. Now shift the weight onto the front foot without turning it out. The back toe is still on the floor, and the foot is turned out. The arms haven't moved. Now, on the change of leg and arms, which is basically the same as in walk #1, bring the back knee in so that the foot will not be turned out by the time you have pointed it forward. The main thing is that the impulse comes from the back heel sliding on the floor, turning the back foot out, and pushing the forward hip and leg forward. It is a highly stylized classic walk, that should only be used when the character you are playing would walk that way.

If homework assignments have been brought in, look at them.

If there is time, do some duets.

Homework Assignment: Bring in a short exercise, using the chest impulses for every arm movement.

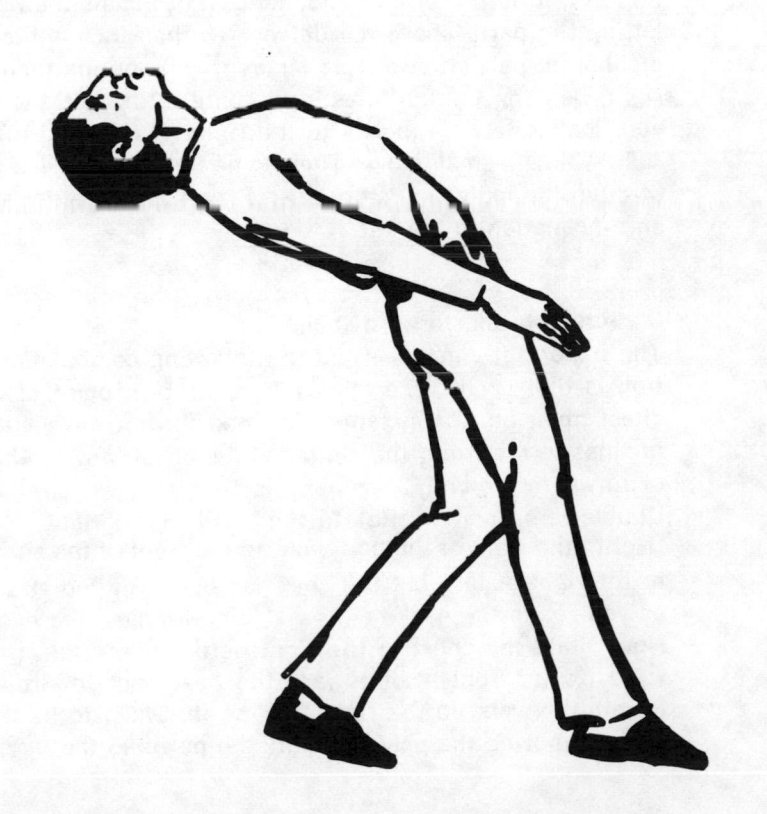

LESSON TWELVE

Inclinations; rotations; combinations of inclinations and rotations involving two directions; beginning and advanced hand exercises; balance exercises including the forward inclination; climbing stairs; climbing a rope; comic walks.

82   Run through the inclinations and rotations a couple of times.

Combinations of Inclinations and Rotations: The combinations have a dual purpose: one is to develop more and finer control of the various parts of the body; the other is to eventually be able to fall into the final combination positions without going through the intermediate steps.

1. Inclination forward, and inclination to the side.
Stand in the double-zero position. Incline just the head forward; keep the point of the chin where it is, and incline the head to its right (be sure the neck doesn't move). Incline the neck forward (keeping what you have achieved with the head); now incline the neck to its right without moving the chest. Next, incline the chest forward (keeping the position of the neck and head in the same relationship with the chest, so that they move with it); then incline the chest to its right, toward the right shoulder. Next, incline the waist forward, to its front, letting the parts above it ride with it; then incline the waist to its right. Now incline the pelvis forward as far as it will go; and then incline the pelvis to its right, bending the left knee, and going to the half-toe of the left foot. Be sure you don't rotate the pelvis to the right (it will tend to): The inclination to the right will be a small move. Then come up smoothly and gradually (without going through the individual steps). Now try it on the other side: inclination forward, and inclination to the left.

2. Rotation and forward inclination.
The important concept in all the following combinations which include a rotation is that each piece moves from its own point of view. That is, when the chest must be, for instance, inclined forward, even if it is rotated around, it inclines to the front, the center of the chest; not to where the head is pointing or to where the body in general is facing.
Double-zero position. Rotate the head to the right. Incline the head forward. (Not to the front of the body, but to the front of the head, so that it doesn't lean to the right or left, but the chin has been lowered straight forward.) Keep this as you rotate the neck to the right; now incline the neck forward (to its front). Now rotate the chest to the right, letting the arms rise. Incline the chest forward (to its front—not toward the head, not toward the front of the body). Rotate the waist to the right. Incline the waist to its front, as far as it will go without moving the pelvis. Rotate the pelvis to the right, bending the left knee.

Incline the pelvis forward, to its front, as far as it will go. Come up slowly and smoothly.

You may notice that the final positions of many of the combinations look like the drawings on Greek vases. That is because the drawings on Greek vases are the human body extended to its maximum in various directions. When Etienne Decroux was inventing these control exercises for mime in the early 1930s, among the areas of his exploration were the Greek vases, and the conclusions he reached about them helped in the development of the inclinations and rotations.

Do it on the other side: Rotate to the left, and incline forward with each piece.

Combinations Two Directions

1. Inclination Forward
Inclination to Side

2. Rotation
Inclination Forward

3. Rotation to the side, and inclination to the same side.
Rotate the head to the right; keep the point of the chin where it is, and incline the head to its right (toward the right ear). Rotate the neck to the right; incline the neck to its right. Rotate the chest to the right, lifting the arms; incline the chest to its right (toward the right shoulder). Rotate the waist to the right; incline the waist to its right. Rotate the pelvis to the right, bending the left knee, and going to the half-toe of the left foot; incline the pelvis a very little bit to its right (be careful that you don't incline the pelvis forward here; it should not be inclined forward at all). Unwind slowly. Do it on the other side: rotation to the left, and inclination to the left for each piece.

4. Rotation to the side, and inclination to the opposite side.
Rotate the head to the right. Keeping the point of the chin where it is, incline the head to its left (toward the left ear). Rotate the neck to the right; incline the neck to its left. Rotate the chest to the right, lifting the arms; incline the chest to its left (toward the left shoulder). Rotate the waist to the right; incline the waist to its left. Rotate the pelvis to the right, bending the left knee, and going to the half-toe of the left foot; incline the pelvis to the left by leaning toward the left knee. Do not incline the pelvis forward here. Unwind slowly. Do it on the other side: rotation to the left, and inclination to the right.
This completes the combinations involving two directions to the front.
For the next group, start in the starting position for a rear inclination, with one foot forward, and the weight between them.

3. *Rotation and Inclination*
   to Same Side

4. *Rotation to Side*
   Inclination to Opposite Side

5. Inclination to the rear and inclination to the side.

Incline the head to the rear. Keep the point of the chin where it is, and incline the head to the left. Keep this, and incline the neck to its rear; incline the neck to its left. Be careful not to move the chest with the neck. Now incline the chest to the rear; and incline the chest to the left. Incline the waist to the rear; incline the waist to the left. Incline the pelvis to the rear by bending the back knee, and keep all the rest in line with it. Now twist around a bit to the left with the pelvis; be sure you do not rotate around as you incline the pelvis: stay parallel to the floor. Come up. Now, keeping the same foot forward that you started with, do the same thing on the other side: inclination to the rear, and inclination to the right. Now change feet, putting the other one forward, and do the whole sequence over: first the inclination to the rear and inclination to the left combination; and then the inclination to the rear and inclination to the right sequence. The balance is different depending on which foot is forward, so that to complete all positions the sequence must be repeated with each foot forward.

5. *Inclination to Rear*
Inclination to Side

6. *Rotation to Side*
Inclination to Rear

6. Rotation to the side, and inclination to the rear.

Start in the starting position for the rear inclination. Rotate the head to the left; incline the head to its rear. Be careful that the head is just lifted, and not inclined toward the front of the body. Rotate the neck to the left; incline the neck to its rear. Rotate the chest to the left, lifting the arms; incline the chest to its rear (towards the center of the back). Rotate the waist to the left, being careful not to move the pelvis yet; incline the waist to its rear. Rotate the pelvis to the left; incline the pelvis to its rear by bending the back knee as far as it will go. Unwind and come up. Do it on the other side; keeping the same foot forward: rotation to the right, and inclination to the rear. Now change feet, and do the whole sequence over. This completes the combinations involving two directions to the rear.

Practice the beginning and the advanced hand exercises.

Balance Exercises: Balance in mime is quite different from balance in dance. Mime balance is achieved by placing the body in certain balanced positions while in a state of relaxation. There is no gripping, no particular tension; the balance has to do with the relationship between the various parts of the body.

1. The simple balance turn.

Stand straight, arms relaxed at your sides. Point the right foot to the side, heel off the floor, with the knee straight. Draw a half-circle on the floor with your toe as you bring the right leg around forward, bending the knee, and ending with the right half-toe as far as it can go behind the left foot. The right toe should be about two inches from the outside of the left foot. Both feet should still be turned out. This movement, enveloping the right foot around to the side of the left should be smooth. This is the starting position for all the balance turns. Start to turn to the left, rising up on both toes as you do, and straightening both knees as you turn. You should be up on the half-toe of both feet, knees straight as you turn. The shin of the right leg, pressing against the shin of the left leg as you rise up and straighten the legs, helps you to turn. The body must remain vertical, without any of its parts rotating: The body must stay in a straight line. If you lead with the pelvis, or incline the chest to the rear a bit, you will lose your balance. Turn all the way around, so you're facing forward again. As you finish the turn, come down on the front foot (the left) which stays straight, bend the back knee (the right knee), and turn the right toe over, so that the pointed right foot is behind the left heel. If you keep your weight a bit forward on this turn, the balance is better. Practice it many times, but never do it very quickly. The purpose is balance, and it's better achieved with a slow turn. Do it on the other side: Point the left to the side, envelope it around the right foot, and turn to the right. Be sure you come down on the front foot as you finish the turn, and bend the back knee, turning the foot over. Check to see that your knees are straight, and that you're way up on the half-toe on the turn.

2. The balance turn with a forward inclination.

Point the right foot straight forward, weight back on the left, and body up straight; look straight ahead. Incline the head forward; incline the neck forward; incline the chest forward; as you incline the waist forward, shift the weight forward onto the right foot; turn the right foot out as you step forward onto it. Be sure the pelvis is still vertical. Point the left leg to the left side, envelope it around the right foot as we did for the simple turn. Now, keeping the weight forward, pelvis straight, turn to the right. Straighten both knees, rise to the half-toe of both feet, but keep the forward inclination of everything down to the waist as you turn. The weight will tend to shift back, which throws you off balance. Focus on the floor in front of you—feel like you're leaning too far forward. As you finish the turn, come down on the front foot, bending the back knee and turning the foot over. You've now completed the turn, but you're still inclined forward. The finish is as follows: Point the left to the side, pull the left leg in next to the right, rising up on the toes of both feet and lifting the chest, the neck, and the head as you do so, the arms rising as the chest lifts, and lower the arms as you lower the heels. Now do the turn on the other side: Start with the left pointed forward, when you're inclined forward, envelope the right around, turn to the left, and the right goes to the side for the finish. Do it several times on each side. If you keep having difficulty maintaining balance, draw an imaginary circle on the floor about four feet away from you, and point at it as you turn. This may help keep the weight forward. Or, try the turn and be looking for something on the floor as you turn. Motivation usually helps.

Balance Exercise

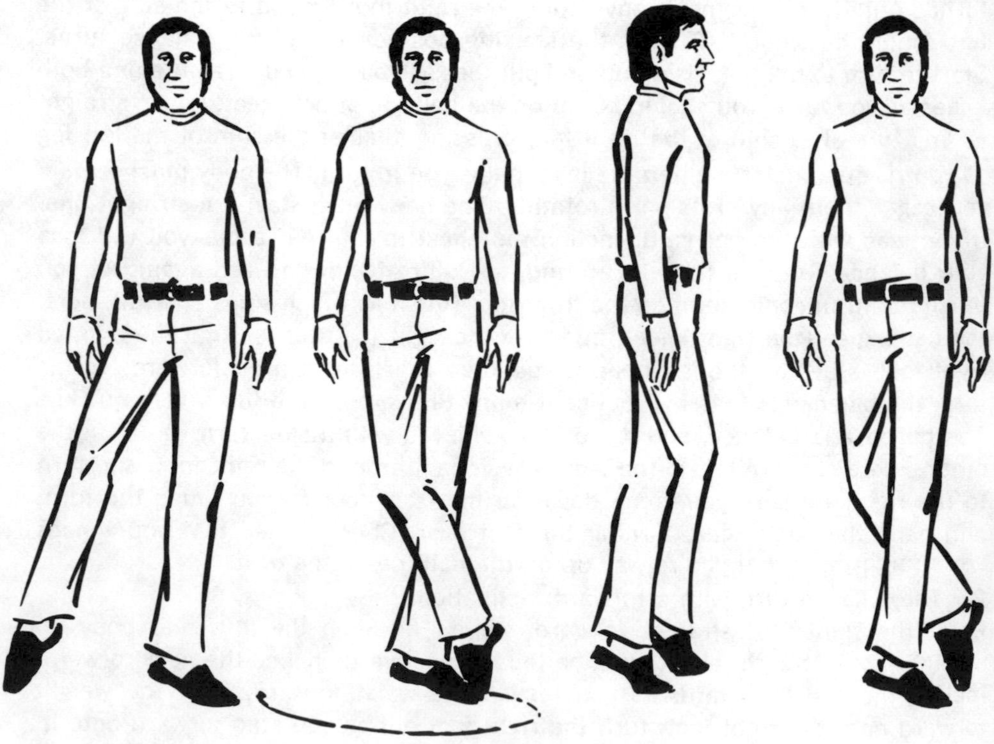

1.   2.

Climbing Stairs: Much of this illusion is given by using an imaginary bannister. Practice the bannister separately: For going up stairs, the hand on the bannister will move from high in front of you, down to near your waist. You can either do the movement in two parts, half of the downward movement for one step, half for the next step, and then reach way up and forward for the next two steps; or you can move your hand a shorter distance, and reach up on each step up. The feet move very much like they do on the imaginary ladder which we climbed in Lesson Six, except that you cover ground, actually moving forward on each step when climbing stairs, and you remain in place when climbing a ladder. The feet: Lift your right foot into the air, as if you were going to put it on the next higher step, and place it on the floor, on its half-toe, a few inches in front of the left. The right knee is now bent. Rise up onto the half-toe of both feet, straightening both knees, and then come down on the right heel, keeping the right knee straight, and bending the left knee, and going to the half-toe of the left foot. Now lift the left foot from the half-toe, place it as if on the next higher step, in front of the right, on its half-toe, rise up on both half-toes, straightening the knees, and come down on the left, bending the right behind. Coordinate the arm movements with this, so that as you rise up, as if climbing, the hand on the bannister moves down. The simultaneous movement of the body up and the arm down will give the illusion of climbing the stairs. Try to feel focused on climbing—try to imagine a real stairway, and picture yourself climbing it—this will help give the illusion.

89

Climbing Stairs #1

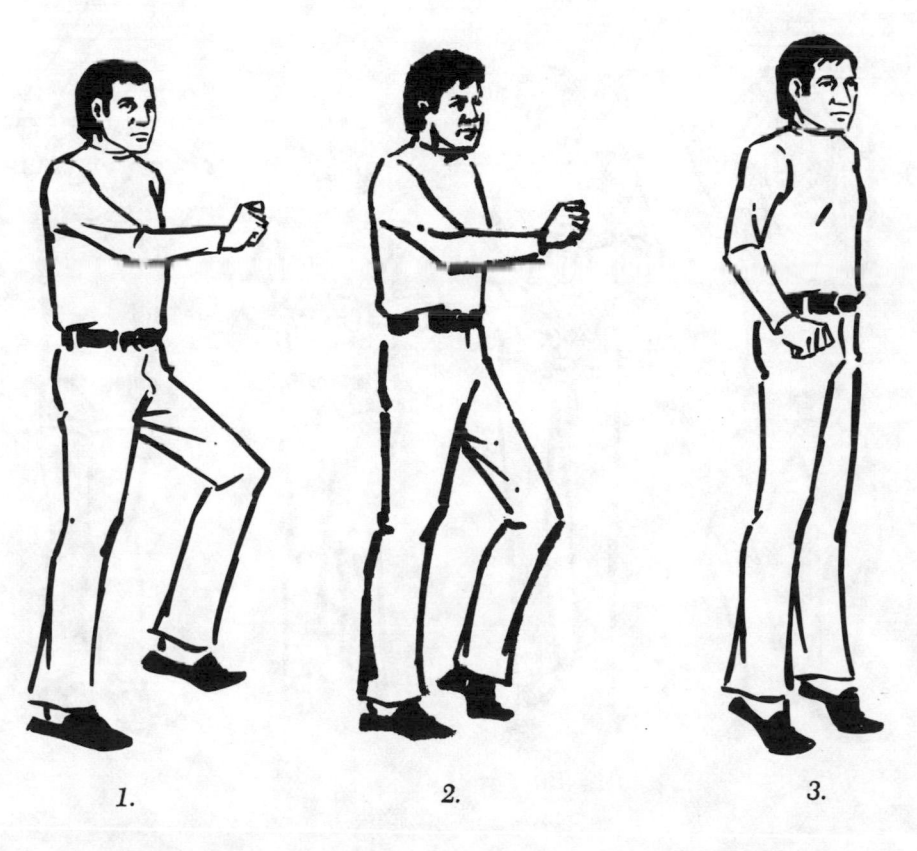

1.   2.   3.

To go downstairs, the feet do exactly the same thing, and the bannister goes from down to up: from reaching down and forward to pulling up to near the waist with the elbow bent. But now your focus must be down: You must feel that you are going down, and the resultant action will be different in the body from climbing up. Practice stair climbing with the left hand on the bannister, and then try it with the right. Try big steps, little steps, long steps, a spiral staircase, etc.

Climbing a Rope: Start with both hands reaching high over your head as if holding onto a rope, both knees bent, and close to each other, and the feet flat on the floor. Slowly, holding on tight, pull your hands straight down in front of you, as if you are pulling yourself up on a rope. At the same time, gradually straighten the knees, and rise up as high as you can go——onto both half-toes. When your hands on the rope are in front of your face, and you are high up on your toes, complete the movement by suddenly grabbing the imaginary rope with your knees, bending the knees, and putting your heels down. During this grab the pull-down continues until the hands on the rope are below your chin. Now reach your left hand as high as you can go and grasp the rope with it, and now reach with the right, and grab. You are in the starting position again. Pull down, rising up, grab with your knees. Continue.

90

Climbing a Rope

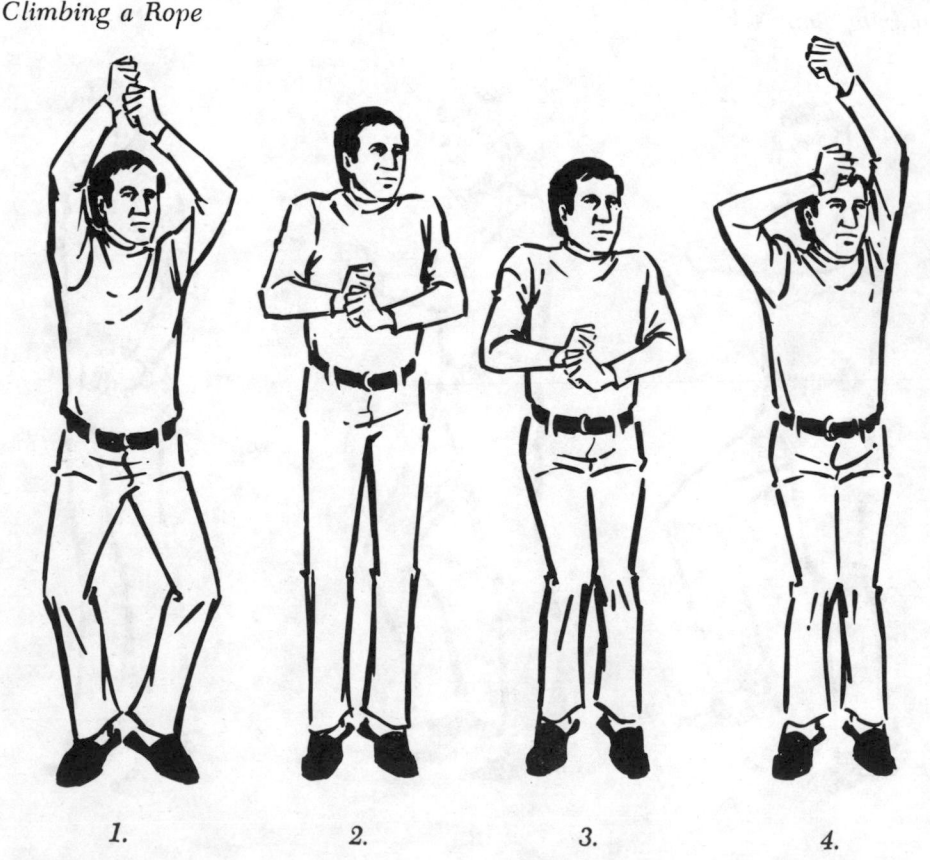

1.   2.   3.   4.

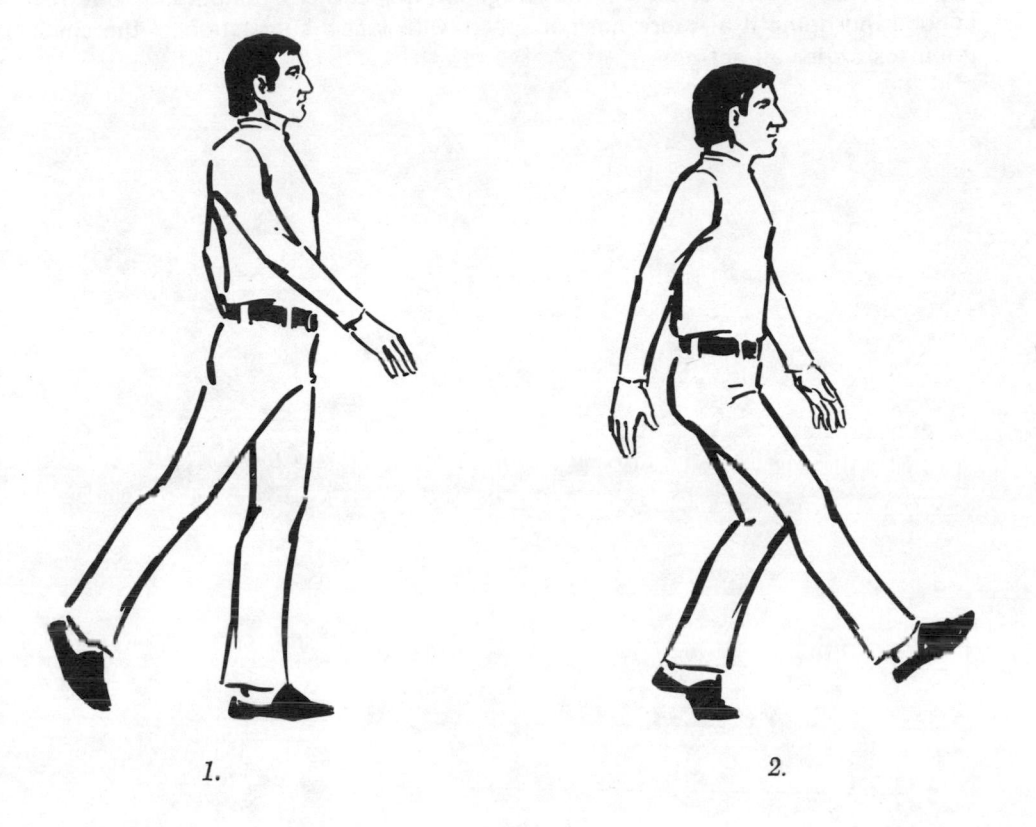

1.   2.

Comic Walks: Start with the weight on the left foot, both knees straight, right leg pointed back, with the toe off the floor, right arm forward. Bring the right leg forward, keeping the knee straight, and as it passes the left foot, bend the left knee and go to the half-toe of the left foot, and change the arms, so that now the right leg, straight, is in the air in front, the left arm is forward, and you are on the half-toe of the left foot, with the left knee bent. Now put the weight on the right foot. Put the whole foot down in one piece (not toe-heel), keeping the right knee straight. Left arm is still forward. Both feet stay turned out for this walk. Now swing the left leg forward, straightening it as it passes the right foot. As it passes, bend the right knee, go to the half-toe of the right foot, and change the arms so that the right arm is now forward, with the flexed left foot in front. Now put the weight down onto the left foot, keeping the knee straight. Be sure you only change the arms when the leg swings forward. Stay upright, and the head should stay level with the floor. Don't bob up and down. Remember, the knee must be straight in front, and it stays straight as you come down on the front foot. The foot stays flexed, not pointed, so that you can come down on the flat of the foot. Try it until it becomes easy. Don't take a very big step, and don't cross one foot in front of the other in front. Now try the same walk without turning out either foot, and with very small steps.

Look at the homework assignments.

Homework Assignment: Diminution. As in the assignment given at the end of Lesson Nine, bring in the same action twice: one time with slow clear chest impulses, and then repeat it, rounding out the corners, smoothing out the action, and doing it at more normal speed, with just a suggestion of the chest impulses under all actions.

Inclinations; rotations; combinations involving three directions; balance exercises with forward inclination; illusory walks #1 and #2; transtation improvisations.

Run through the inclinations and rotations a couple of times.
Do all the combinations involving two directions that we did in Lesson Twelve.

93

Combinations involving three directions:
1. Rotation to one side, inclination forward, and inclination to the same side.
Stand in the double-zero position. Rotate just the head to the right. Incline the head forward, to its front (not to the front of the body). Keep the point of the chin where it is, and incline the head to its right. Rotate the neck to the right; incline the neck to its front; incline the neck to its right. Rotate the chest to the right, lifting the arms, incline the chest forward (to the front, the center of the chest); incline the chest to its right (toward the right shoulder). Rotate the waist to the right, Incline it forward, incline it to its right. Rotate the pelvis to the right, bending the left knee; incline the pelvis forward as far as it will go; incline the pelvis a tiny bit more to its right. Come up slowly, unwinding smoothly. Now do it on the other side: rotation to the left, inclination forward, and inclination to the left of each piece.
2. Rotation to one side, inclination forward, and inclination to the opposite side.
Double-zero position. Rotate the head to the right; incline the head forward (to its front); keep the point of the chin where it is, and incline the head to its left (toward the left ear). Rotate the neck to the right; incline the neck to its front; incline the neck to its left. Rotate the chest to the right, lifting the arms; incline the chest to its front; incline the chest to its left (toward the left shoulder) Rotate the waist to the right; incline the waist forward; incline the waist to its left. Rotate the pelvis to the right; incline the pelvis forward as far as it will go; incline the pelvis a little bit to its left. Unwind smoothly. Do it on the other side: rotation to the left, then inclination forward, then inclination to the right of each part.
3. Rotation to one side, inclination to the rear, inclination to the same side.
Start in the starting position for a rear inclination. Rotate the head to the right; incline the head to the rear by lifting the chin; incline the head to its right (toward the right ear). Rotate the neck to the right; incline the neck to its rear; incline the neck to its right. Rotate the chest to the right, lifting the arms; incline the chest to its rear; incline the chest to its right. Rotate the waist to the right; incline the waist to the rear; incline the waist to its right. Rotate the pelvis to the right; incline the pelvis to the rear as far as it will go; incline the pelvis to its right—go as far as you can go. Unwind up. Try it on the other side: Don't change the foot you have forward. Rotate each piece to the left, incline it to its rear, incline it to its left.

4. Rotation to one side, inclination to the rear, inclination to the opposite side. Put the other foot forward. Rotate the head to the right; incline the head to its rear; incline the head to its left. Rotate the neck to the right; incline the neck to its rear, incline the neck to its left. Rotate the chest to the right, lifting the arms; incline the chest to its rear; incline the chest to its left. Rotate the waist to the right; incline the waist to the rear; incline the waist to its left. Rotate the pelvis to the right; incline it to the rear as far as it will go; incline the pelvis to its left. Come up—unwind slowly. Now try it on the other side (but don't change the foot that is forward). If you want to get all possible combinations, you'd have to do all four rear combinations with the left foot forward, and then all four with the right forward. But I think four is enough, so keep one foot forward for the first two, and the other for the remaining two.

94   *Combinations Three Directions*

1. Rotation to One Side
Inclination Forward
Inclination to Same Side

2. Rotation to One Side
Inclination to Rear
Inclination to Same Side

3. Rotation to One Side
Inclination Forward
Inclination to Opposite Side

4. Rotation to One Side
Inclination to Rear
Inclination to Opposite Side

Practice the balance exercises we did in Lesson Twelve, including the forward inclination.

Practice illusory walks #1 and #2, first doing the two separate halves of each walk, then developing into the walks.

Do the transtation improvisations we did in Lesson One.

Look at the homework.

Homework Assignment: Bring in a short sketch based on an object. The way to prepare this is to take any imaginary object, such as a beer bottle, and start working with it. Perhaps the top won't come off; maybe it sprays you when it does; maybe there's nothing in the bottle—you won't know what will happen until you improvise with the object. Then try improvising with another imaginary object. Then try a third one. Then pick the best of your three improvisations, and develop it: Add things, follow your ideas. You don't have to **write** a sketch, let it come out of improvisations. But for this homework assignment, the object should set off your sketch, and should be the central figure. Keep it short—about one minute or less.

The body as a unit; improvisations with the body as a unit; duos with the body as a unit.

Do all the exercises we did in Lesson Five: the forward and side tilts; the unit knee bends; the scale-fulcrum tilts; the sways; the walks; and have each person individually do an improvisation based on the body as a unit. Let them practice a few minutes before performing the improvisations.

Duos with the Body as a Unit: Assign a partner to each person, and have them practice a short sketch with two characters. They must keep the body as a unit for today. (This exercise can be done without keeping the body as a unit on another day.)
Look at homework.

Homework Assignment: Bring in a sketch that you have practiced that keeps the body as a unit.

LESSON FIFTEEN

Inclinations; rotations; rotation turns; pelvic impulse exercises; beginning and advanced hand exercises; improvisations with pelvic impulses.

Do the inclinations and rotations a few times.

Rotation Turns: The rotation turn is a continuation of the rotation that takes you all the way around in a complete circle. Rotate to the right: head, neck, chest, waist, pelvis. Now bend the right knee, and at the same time slide the right heel forward as far as you can. The toe stays in place on the floor, and everything stays in line and keeps turning to the right. Don't slide the foot on the floor, just push the heel forward. Now, keeping the feet still on the floor, twist the body around further to the right, keeping the weight on the right foot, and keeping the right knee bent. Now envelope the left leg around forward in a half-circle (as we did in the balance exercises) until it rests on its half-toe near the outside of the right foot. Now turn, straightening both knees and rising on the half-toe of both feet, until you are facing forward again with your heels together. Come down, lowering the heels and the arms. Practice it several times on each side, slowly, being sure not to leave out the middle step, where you twist further to the side you are turning before enveloping the foot around. Now try it smoothly, as a continuation of a smooth rotation, without stopping between steps: Make it as if you are looking for something, and perhaps find it in the front of the room.

Do all the pelvic impulse exercises that we did in Lesson Seven, including the illusions of pushing and pulling.

Practice the beginning and advanced hand exercises.

Perform an improvisation that you have practiced for a few minutes using pelvic impulses.

Look at the homework.

Homework Assignment: Bring in a sketch that uses some of the pelvic impulses in it.

LESSON SIXTEEN

Transtations; advanced rope-pulling; up and down stairs; up and down a ladder; up and down a rope; beginning and advanced hand exercises; facial exercises; comic walks; eye improvisations.

Do all the transtations.

Advanced Rope-Pulling: Start with the feet wide apart. Bend the left knee and tilt the body over to the left as you would with the body as a unit, with everything in line with the straight right leg. Place your hands as if they are holding on to an imaginary rope which is at waist level. Look to the left, as if towards the other end of the rope. Your hands should be about a foot and a half to two feet apart, and close to your body—not extended—both elbows bent. Leave a space in your hands for the thickness of the rope. This is the starting position and the finishing position for the pull.

The first move is to cross the right hand over the left, grasping the rope just in front of the left hand. Now reach the left hand further along the rope, so that you grasp it about a foot and a half further along; but do not reach so far that your left elbow is straight: It should still be bent. The body has not moved yet. Next, leading with the right hip, and bending the right knee as you go, pull to the right: pelvis, and then chest, straightening the left arm as you do so, and shifting all the weight onto the right leg. Your body is now in line with the left leg, which has straightened, and your arms are extended to the left, the right knee bent. Next, at the same time, pull the rope in, lead with the left hip, bending the left knee, and shift the weight to the left: pelvis, and then chest. The pulling in of the rope should coincide with the shift to the left, and you should end in the same position in which you started the sequence. Repeat it many times slowly until it becomes smooth—when it does, the time to stop is between sequences, letting the rest run together. It is most important to straighten the arms only while pulling away. There will be a tendency to bend the elbows and pull in while pulling away, but this will spoil the illusion. Pull in only while moving toward your imaginary opponent. Do it on the other side.

Practice going up and down stairs as we did in Lesson Twelve.

Practice climbing up a ladder as we did in Lesson Six.

1.

2.

3.

4.

5.

Down a Ladder: The coordination of this exercise is quite difficult because the timing is different for the hands and the feet. It is best to practice the hands and feet separately, and then try to put them together.

The feet: Stand straight; reach the right leg back, as if you were going to walk backwards; let the knee bend as you reach, and then straighten as it reaches as far as it will go. Keep the knee straight, bring the leg back in, and at the same time go to the half-toe of the left foot bending the left knee. Now reach the left foot back, saying "Reach" to yourself, and as you bring it back in straight, while you bend the right knee and go to the half-toe of the right foot, say "In," Keep alternating, saying "Reach . . . in" as you do it.

The hands: Start with your hands on the imaginary rungs, the left higher. Now, as you climb down, the right hand will have to travel up about ten inches. First, let go with the left, and as it moves down to the rung below the one the right is on, the right moves up (still grasping the rung) about five inches; the left takes hold of its rung ten inches below the right, and they both move up the remaining five inches together. The difficult part is that the hand that is moving up is doing its move at a different speed from the one that is going down. It moves up slowly for five inches, while the other goes down fifteen inches in the same time, and then they finish the upward move together. As you move the right up and the left down, say "Reach," and as you move them both the final five inches say "In," to correspond with the movements of the feet. The hand moving up does not stop at five inches—it continues, and the hand that grasps below it joins it for the final move. Keep ten inches between them at all times.

The whole thing is: Right hand moving up, left hand moving down, and left leg reaching back; leg is as far back as it can go as the left hand grasps the lower rung (same hand and leg for going down) ("Reach"); left leg pulls in straight, while the right knee bends and you go to the half-toe of the right, and at the same time both hands, grasping their rungs, move up the final five inches ("In"). Now right hand and leg reaching down as the left, holding the rung, moves up its five inches, then "In" as the right leg moves in, and the hands continue up. It's tricky, but if you keep trying, doing the two parts separately, you should eventually get it. Meanwhile, in an emergency, you can do the legs as described, and hold the two sides of the ladder, and just slide your hands up as you climb down.

Climb a rope as we did in Lesson Twelve.

Try **climbing down a rope,** by doing the opposite: let the arms go up as the knees open, and grab them closed as your arms are extended over your head. Then place the hands, one at a time on the rope down near your chest, open the knees, and let the arms go way up then grab with the knees again.

Do the beginning and advanced hand exercises (Lesson Three and Lesson Eleven).

Do the comic walks as in Lesson Twelve.

Run through the facial exercises.

Do the eye improvisations we did in Lesson Three.

Do some kind of an improvisation using climbing and/or pulling.

Look at the homework.

Homework Assignment: Bring in a short sketch based on a place. Pick any environment, such as a pool hall, and start working on it: Use the objects in the place, explore the place, and see what actions the place dictates—there can be a juke box, a pool table, a telephone booth, a coke machine, anything you might find in the environment. Then pick another place, like the beach, or the kitchen. Let the place provoke all your actions. Do three of these improvisatons, and pick the best one to elaborate on. As with the object sketch, don't try to write the piece—improvise it, and then re-do it. Keep it short.

LESSON SEVENTEEN

Inclinations; rotations; combinations involving two and three directions; balance exercise with forward inclination; walks #1 and #2; illusory walks #1 #2; illusory run.

Do the inclinations and rotations.
Do the combinations involving two directions as in Lesson Twelve.
Do the ones involving three directions as in Lesson Thirteen.
Do the balance exercise including the forward inclination as in Lesson Twelve.
Do walk #1—Lesson One, and walk #2—Lesson Eleven.
Do illusory walk #1—Lesson Four, and illusory walk #2—Lesson Nine.
Practice the illusory run—Lesson Ten.
Look at the homework.

Homework Assignment: Bring in a one-minute sketch that has an illusion in it —such as walking in place, climbing, pulling, pushing, tugging, stairs, running, etc.

LESSON EIGHTEEN

Animal characterizations; improvisations with two animal characters; projection into an object.

Do the animal characterization exercise we did in Lesson Eight. First do two animals and perform them for the group. Then evolve them up into animallike people and perform these characters for the group, but this time, don't have them speak: Have them perform the same action—that is, each person's two animal-characters can select an action such as planting flowers or trying on clothes, and do it first as one of his characters, and then the same action as the other character, so we can see the difference. Each person should select his own action for his characters.

Now, pair off, and practice a sketch involving two characters. Each person should use one of the two animal-characters that he has practiced. If there is an odd person, one group can be a trio. After practicing this, they should be performed for the group.

Projection into an Object: In this exercise you either become an object, or part of you becomes an object while the rest of you uses it. There is an old print of an early Pierrot that you can see in Pierre DuChartre's book **Italian Comedy** which shows the actor using his lower leg and foot as a gun: With his knee brought up against his chest he is sighting along the lower leg. In Marcel Marceau's piece "In the Park," there is a moment when he is sweeping the ground, and uses his leg and foot as the broom. So there are present in these both the man and the object he is using. With the next step, becoming the object, the man using it is not present—only the object. When I do a piece of bacon frying in a pan, I shrivel as bacon does. You can be a washing machine, a pair of scissors, a piano, an orange-drink machine, a sewing machine, anything. When you do these, try to capture an attitude for the object as well as the action. How does the washing machine feel about the clothes that are put in it —perhaps it sneezes when the soap is poured in. Give your objects personality. Practice for a few minutes, and then let each person perform his. Spend the rest of the class doing these.

Look at the homework.

Homework Assignment: Bring in a short sketch based on a character. Approach this the same way as we did the sketch based on a place and on an object: Start with the character, and improvise a series of actions for him. Then do another character, and then a third. Pick the best one and develop it. Keep it short.

Inclinations; rotations; rotation turns; balance turns with side and back inclinations; up and down a ladder; comic walks; walk with a high knee; heavy and light objects (counterpoise); improvisations; duets.

104 Do the inclinations and rotations.
Do the rotation turns as in Lesson Fifteen.
Do the balance exercises as in Lesson Twelve, including the forward inclination.

The Balance Turn with Side Inclination: Point the right foot forward as you did when starting the turn with the forward inclination. The weight is back on the left, body up straight, looking straight forward. Incline the head to the right, incline the neck to the right, incline the chest to the right, and as you incline the waist to the right, step forward onto the right foot with all the weight, and turn the right foot out. Point the left foot to the left side, envelope it around the right, just as in all balance turns. Now turn, keeping the side inclination. You will tend to fall to the left: Keep the weight leaning to the right as you go around. Finish the turn, and you should still be inclined to the right. Point the left to the left side, then pull the left leg in, as you straighten the body up to the center, rise on the toes of both feet, lift the arms, and then lower the arms and the heels at the same time. Now, keeping the same starting position, right leg pointed forward, do the same thing with an inclination to the left. Now try it both ways with the left leg pointed forward. The body tries to compensate for the inclination by leaning in the direction opposite from the inclination. Don't let it, or you will lose your balance.

Balance Turn with Rear Inclination: Point the right leg forward; incline the head to the rear, the neck to the rear, the chest to the rear, and as you incline the waist to the rear, step forward onto the right foot, turning it out. Point the left foot to the side, envelope it around the right foot, and do the turn keeping the rear inclination. You will tend to fall forward, so keep leaning back to keep the balance. Finish in a similar manner to the other balance turns. Try it with the left foot forward at the start.

These balances are difficult, and the side ones tend to make you dizzy. If you get dizzy, there's a cure: Stand straight, and bounce your heels hard against the floor, jarring your whole body. Dizziness is caused by unequal levels of the water in the semi-circular canals in the ears—when you jar the body, the water tends to level out, restoring your equilibrium. You can do the same thing if you have been spinning around and lose your balance. Just jounce the body, and you'll regain it.

Practice going up and down a ladder—Lesson Six and Lesson Sixteen.

Do the comic walks—Lesson Twelve.
Practice the walk with a high knee—Lesson Nine.

Heavy and Light Objects (Counterpoise): In carrying a heavy object you must
lean in the opposite direction to give the illusion. This is called counterpoise.
If you are carrying a heavy suitcase in the right hand, you must lean way over to
the left to give the impression that it is heavy. Same with a full bucket of water,
or anything else that's supposed to be heavy. Use all the energy you would
use if the object were real: Your muscles should strain just as much with the
imaginary object. If you are carrying a heavy bundle in front of you, lean back.
You may notice that pregnant women tend to lean back to balance the weight
they are carrying in front. If you have something heavy on your back, you must
lean forward, or you'll fall over backwards. If you must carry two suitcases, lift
them, and pull your shoulders down, so that it looks like the weight of the
suitcases is pulling you down. Strain a lot, and it'll look more real. If you are
picking up an empty suitcase or bucket, you don't lean or strain.
Try handling very tiny imaginary objects: Put lead in a pencil, set a small watch,
put a flint in a lighter, etc. Practice giving thickness to even the smallest
objects.
Do some improvisations that include some kind of a turn, and the handling of
heavy or light objects.
Look at the homework.
Do some duets—Lesson Four.

Homework Assignment: Bring in a one-minute sketch.

105

Mirror exercise; age and youth; occupations; where-from-where-to game; object transformations; building a machine.

This class has to do with utilization of the techniques we have learned so far. Do the mirror exercise we did in Lesson Six.

106

Age and Youth: Have each person practice being a particular age. Pick a specific year, like ten years old or forty-three or seventy-one. Don't just pick old, or teen-age, or young—be specific. Try to find the unique qualities of each age. Little babies, when they just start to walk, turn out their arms and legs, after a few years, these straighten; older, and the body is limper, looser; into the twenties, it starts to be pulled into place; the hardest is finding differences in the years from twenty-five to forty-five, but there are some you can find. Then aging starts, and the body gradually becomes a bit stiffer, it's harder to bend over as you near sixty; as you get really old, don't do the cliche of the hand on the hip, the bent frame, and the cane—try to achieve the result without the props. See how old you can get. After each one has practiced an age, let him perform them for the group, and have the group guess how old he was trying to be. The one who performed it should not tell how old he tried for until everyone has guessed. Then, have everyone try another, different, age, and perform it.

Occupations: Try to be a character who has a particular occupation. What we want to see here is not the depiction of the occupation itself (such as putting on fins and jumping into the water for a skin diver), but the effect of the occupation on the body, and how it moves. The watchmaker may bend forward a bit and perhaps squint; the boxer has a way of walking related to his occupation (don't show him sparring or shadow-boxing—show him doing something else); a nun will have a different look about her from a hooker. Don't be blatant: Try for subtlety. Have each person practice and then perform for the group, and have the group guess what his occupation is. Try another one.

Where-from-Where-to: This is a game that was invented by Viola Spolin, and is found in her book **Improvisation for the Theatre.** (The mirror exercise and similar age and occupation exercises may also be found in her book, but are not unique to her.) It is a game form that has particular interest to mimes, since the action is communicated only physically, and unless you can define an environment, and handle objects with clarity, you will not fulfill the obligations of the game: You will not communicate your story.

The idea is to show where you are coming from, and where you are going to, without actually depicting those places—by doing some action in the interim between the two places that will show both. For instance, if you enter as if shaking water off yourself, dry yourself with a towel, dress in a costume, put on stage makeup and a beard, check your lines in a script, clear your throat, and exit, you are going from the shower to the stage. You have not shown the shower (only its aftereffect) and you have not shown the stage (only the preparation for it). The scene in the dressing room shows where you have been and where you are going. Another example might be to start suspended in a parachute. You create the feeling of floating down, the plane flies off into the distance; you look down, become alarmed, pull on the cords of the chute, unhook something at your waist, bring a tube to your mouth, and blow up something that inflates at your waist. You tie it off, look down some more, and hold your breath. You are going from an airplane to the water—and you have shown neither the plane nor the water, only the interim which shows both. You can become abstract if you want, doing things like from heaven to hell, from the frying pan to the fire, or you can do random ones—picking any two places. One that I did that was suggested by an audience member who wrote it down and passed it up was "From a nudist colony to a monastery." Try it. Better yet, try your own. Each person should do one or two of these.

Object Transformations: This is another of Viola Spolin's "Theatre Games. Have the group stand in a circle. Have one person start with any object that has a physical activity involved with its use, such as a pencil sharpener. Do the action of sharpening a pencil, and then gradually let the motion change; let it drift away from the pencil-sharpening motion, gradually changing form, tempo, distance, etc., until you are doing an abstract motion. Let it keep changing, gradually, until you reach a point where you realize you are handling a new object. The next person in the circle will start with the new object (perhaps it has become a conductor's baton), and will do the movement, and then gradually let it change until there is no object, and then further, until he is handling a new object. Then pass it on to the next person.

Don't think while you do this. Don't say to yourself "Oh, this is something like conducting with a baton," and then do the action of the baton. Rather watch your body do the action, wondering what it will do, and wait until you **realize** what you are handling now. If you think, and then go toward what you see coming, you will miss the moment of realization, which is what the game is about.

You can pass this around the circle many times. If it is a large group, you can split into small circles of three or four—so everyone gets lots of chances. If you are alone, keep going until you get tired. Be sure you keep the thickness of your objects, and always have an object that you arrive at. Don't end up just doing an activity without an object, such as walking.

Building a Machine: Have one person start an abstract pattern of action in the center of the room. Let the next person take his impetus from one of the movements of the first one, and develop a pattern of his own, related to the first; let the next join onto the first two, and continue until everyone is part of the machine. Try to relate your action to some part of someone else's action (if his hand swings out every three seconds, perhaps that is your cue to duck). Build a couple of different machines.

Look at the homework.

Homework Assignment: If you are on the quarter system this will be the last class of the term before the final, and the final should be a three to five minute sketch that you have created, and which you have practiced to the point where it is performable: Whatever you have to do, whatever illusion is needed to tell your story, should be clear and clean.

If this is not the last class before finals, bring in a couple of where-from-where-to's that you have practiced.

Inclination and rotation of each piece separately; beginning and advanced hand exercises; stairs; merry-go-round; rowing a boat; creating an environment.

Do the inclinations and rotations of each part separately as in Lesson Six.
Do the beginning hand exercises—Lesson Three—and the advanced ones—Lesson Eleven.
Climb up and down stairs—Lesson Twelve.

108

The Merry-Go-Round: It is best to practice this in separate parts, and then put them together. First, stand straight, heels together, and bend the knees, keeping the heels on the floor. Don't try to go low—just as far as you can go without bending the body—this is a plie. With a count of 1, 2, 3, straighten the knees and rise way up on the half-toe of both feet, with the next 1,2,3, lower the heels, and bend the knees again. Do it with a waltz feeling. Up, up, up, down, down, down. Try to move smoothly, taking the full three counts to complete the distance, rather than up on 1, and then holding on 2 and 3. Do it many times. Now have the group make a circle facing counterclockwise (which is the way merry-go-rounds go), plie (knees bent, heels on floor), and move forward, counting up, up, up, down, down, down, as you travel around the circumference of the circle, so you go three steps up, and three steps down. The distance you go up and down is very small on each step, and you will tend to do it all on the first step. The steps should be equal—only rising or lowering a couple of inches on each step. Try to make it smooth: You are trying to give the illusion of the up and down smooth curve you would follow on the seat of a merry-go-round. Practice this until it is smooth and even. The circle will tend to get smaller: Don't let it.
Now for the hands. On a real merry-go-round the hands move up when the body moves up, and down when you go down. But this does not give the illusion well enough, so we do it in opposition. Practice the hands separately: Grasp the imaginary pole in front of your forehead, leaving space for its thickness. On a count of three pull your hands down to the center of your chest, and then on three, up to your forehead again. The distance traveled is short. Don't reach way over your head, and don't go down to the waist. On up, up, up, the hands pull down; on down, down, down, they move up. Do it several times.
First put it together without moving forward: Plié, put your hands at your forehead, and as you rise up, up, up, pull the hands down smoothly to the center of the chest; as you plie smoothly down, down, down, let the hands move up to in front of the forehead. Do this in place several times until it is smooth. Now try it moving around the circle. Get a waltz rhythm going. After everyone has it smoothly, let each alternate person go up as the next one goes down, and you have the complete illusion.

Rowing a Boat: Sit as if in a boat, with one foot a bit forward. Grasp the imaginary oars in front of you. The motion you make with the hands is a circular one that goes from your waist to your knees to your nose to your waist, etc. When your hands are down the oars are out of the water, when they're up, the oars are in the water. There is no resistance when they're out, and lots of resistance from the water when they're in. So do the pull towards you strongly, with effort, and the move of the hands down, and away from you with less effort. The knees stay bent. Do this many times, until you get the feel of it.

To cover ground with this illusion, as your hands reach down and forward, lean forward, and let your right foot step back about eighteen inches or two feet. As you pull the oars in towards you (with the effort) pull the left foot in next to the right one as you sit up, but keep your knees bent so that it looks like you're sitting. Keep doing this. When everyone has it, form boats with several people in them, and row around the room, each person taking his cue from the one in front of him.

Look at homework.

Rowing a Boat

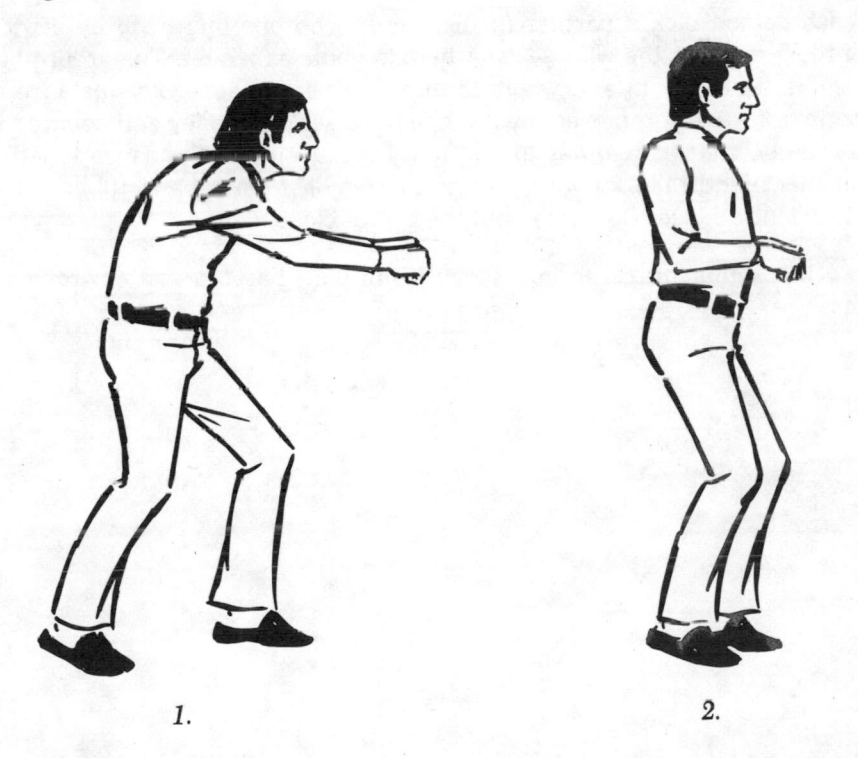

1.   2.

Creating an Environment: Have each person practice exploring an environment: Pick some kind of place—a room, a park, anyplace, and try to find all the things in it, and use them. No story or plot: just showing the environment. Have each person show his. Then pick one and have several people enter the defined environment and use the things in it. Try another one or two. Do this until the end of class time.

Homework Assignment: Bring in an environment, such we have just practiced— no plot: just definition of the place.

Inclinations; rotations; rotation turns; balance exercises with forward, side, and rear inclinations; transtations; where-from-where-to game with two people.

110

Do the inclinations and rotations.
Do the rotation turns—Lesson Fifteen.
Do the balance turns—Lessons Twelve and Nineteen.
Do the transtations.
Look at homework.
Have each person pick a partner (if there is an odd one there can be a trio), and let them practice the where-from-where-to game as a duet. The group then has to guess where from and where to after the performance. For instance, if they came in furtively, removed masks, opened a sack of money and counted it, put guns away, changed clothes to very fancy dress, practiced a dance together for a moment, and then left, they might be coming from a bank robbery and going to a fancy dance. Do these until the end of class time.

Homework Assignment: Bring in a sketch (with plot) based on an environment or place.

LESSON TWENTY-THREE

Inclinations; rotations; combinations involving three directions; balance exercises with forward, side, and rear inclinations; four walks with a high knee; improvisations with a sneaky walk.

Do the inclinations and rotations.

Do the combinations of inclinations involving two directions—Lesson Twelve, and three directions—Lesson Thirteen.

Do the balance exercises with the forward, side, and rear inclinations—Lessons Twelve and Nineteen.

Practice the first walk with a high knee—Lesson Nine. In this version the body remains straight up and down as you sneak forward. The other three high-knee walks are exactly the same from the waist down, but the upper body shifts position. The second one: Start straight up as in the first one, but as you lift the knee for step 2, lean forward with the upper body as far as you can, and as you extend your foot for step 3, extend the opposite arm even further forward. Stay bent forward through step 6, and then as you straighten the bottom leg, changing the arms and lifting the knee, straighten the body up—you're up on 1 and bent forward on 2 through 6. Always be sure the standing leg is straight on 1, and stay bent forward through 6, only straightening on 1.

The third walk with a high knee is the opposite in form to the second. Remember that they are all the same from the waist down. For the third one, start with the body bent forward on step 1, and straighten it as you proceed into steps 2 and 3. Keep the body upright through step 6, and then as you change the arms and lift the other knee, bend the body forward on step 1. Be sure the bottom leg is straight on step 1—it will tend to bend in this version of the walk. You're bent forward on step 1, and up straight on 2 through 6.

The fourth walk with a high knee keeps the body bent forward for all 6 steps. Once again, be sure the bottom leg straightens on step 1. The four walks suggest different characters and different situations, and can be employed in sketches when needed with more or less stylization as the situation and character demand.

Have each person in the group practice a short improvisation which includes sneaking.

Look at homework.

Homework Assignment: Bring in a sketch based on an object. Let the object be your jumping-off place for the improvisation that develops your sketch.

Inclinations; rotations; transtations; advanced rope-pulling; up and down a ladder; illusory walks #1 and #2; being a machine; building a machine; growing; animals evolving.

Do the inclinations, rotations, and transtations.
Practice the advanced rope-pulling—Lesson Sixteen.
Practice going up and down a ladder—Lessons Six and Sixteen.
Practice illusory walk #1—Lesson Four; and illusory walk #2—Lesson Nine.

Being a Machine: As we did in projection into an object, Lesson Eighteen, have each person practice being a machine. The important factors this time are the action, timing, and movement of the machine, rather than the personality. Get several movements going, preferably with contrasting rhythms. Have each person perform his.
Do building a machine, as in Lesson Twenty.

Growing: Have each person practice this: Start as a seed (or nut or fruit) and gradually grow up into your physical impression of the adult plant. Perform these.

Animals Evolving: Have each person practice this: Start as a lower animal, such as a lizard, snake, fish, insect, frog, etc., do the activities of this animal for a while, and then, gradually, evolve into a higher animal such as a dog, cat, elephant, camel, bird, ape, squirrel, etc., and then do the activities of the higher animal. Have each perform his evolution.
Look at homework.

Homework Assignment: Bring in a sketch based on a character.

Inclinations; rotations; pelvis exercises including pushing and pulling; illusory walk backwards; climbing stairs #2; descending stairs backwards; ladder #2; walk #2; walking on the moon; improvisations.

Do the inclinations and rotations.
Practice the pelvic impulse exercises—Lesson Seven.

The Illusory Walk Backwards: The legs are the same as they are in climbing down a ladder: you reach back with the right leg, as if you were going to step backwards—let the knee bend as you reach back, and straighten as you reach its back limit. Keep the right knee straight, bring the leg in, placing the foot on the floor next to the left foot, as you go to the half-toe of the left, bending the left knee. Now reach the left leg back, bring it in, and go to the half-toe of the right as you bring the left in. It is just like the step you would take walking backwards.
The arms are a bit easier with this walk than they are when you go forward: As you reach the right leg back, bring the same arm forward, and keep it going forward until the right foot is in place next to the left. As you reach the left leg back, bring the left arm forward, until the left completes its move. Keep going. Try first walking forward, and then backward.

Stairs #2: There is another way to give the illusion of climbing stairs besides the way we did it in Lesson Twelve. The bannister, of course, remains the same, with the hand reaching from up to down as you climb up. The feet: Place the right foot in the air in front of you about seven inches off the floor, with the foot parallel to the floor, and the lower leg perpendicular. It is as if it is resting on the next step. Rise up onto the half-toe of the left foot, keeping the knee straight, and at the same time straighten the right knee. The moment the right knee is straight, come forward onto the right foot, putting the weight on it, bending the left knee, and staying on the left half-toe. Now lift the left foot onto the next step in front of you, being sure the foot is parallel to the floor. Then rise up onto the half-toe of the right (with the right knee straight) while straightening the left knee—then fall forward onto the left, while bending the right knee. Keep going, but always stop for a fraction of a moment when you place the foot on the next step. You need the stop to establish the step, and then climb. Try it with the arms. Always actually step forward, covering ground with stairs. If you are going to go down stairs, you cannot use this method—use the method described in Lesson Twelve. You can use this, however, for . . .

Descending Stairs Backwards: The bannister will go from down to up as you do this. Step back into the air with your right foot as if you are going to go down a step, bending the right knee; step onto the right foot behind you, straightening the knee, and as you do so, lift the foot into the air in front of you about seven inches off the floor, with the foot parallel to the floor, and the lower leg perpendicular to the ground. The end position is the same as the starting position for stairs #2. You do cover ground, moving back across the floor with this climb. Keep going, letting the bannister move as the foot rises in the front. Try going up and down.

Ladder #2: This is the same principle as stairs #2: Place the right foot on the imaginary rung of the ladder. With the ladder you do not cover ground, moving forward as you do with the stairs: You stay in one spot. As you place the foot, say "Place," as you put it on the ground while bending the left and going to the left half-toe, say "Climb"—and now coordinate it with the hands exactly as you did with the other ladder climb in Lesson Six. Once again, use opposite hand and foot going up, and the same hand and foot going down. Yes, you can try the ladder down just as we did the stairs descending backwards, but don't cover ground—stay in one spot.

Practice walk #2—Lesson Thirteen.

Walking on the Moon: Step forward onto the half-toe of the right foot, with the right knee bent and the left knee straight. Place the right half-toe about sixteen inches in front of the left foot and a little off to the right. Left arm forward, right arm back. Put the weight on the right half-toe, and as the weight goes onto it, straighten the knee, so that you are balanced way up on the right half-toe, and the left comes off the floor. When you reach the top, put the right heel down and bend the right knee—the left is still off the floor in back. What you want is a feeling of weightlessness, so you continually float up and down as you walk forward. The left leg now floats higher in back, and you straighten the right knee and then bend it again as the left drifts higher.

Now change the leg and arms: The left leg floats forward as the right arm goes forward and the left arm back. As you do the change, straighten and then bend the right knee; it is bent as you finish the change. You are now ready for the next step.

Step onto the half-toe of the left, shift the weight to the left, straightening the knee and staying way up on the half-toe, then put the heel down and bend the knee. Straighten and then bend the left knee as the right leg drifts higher in the back, and then straighten and bend the left again as you do the change of leg and arms . . . continue. Try to feel weightless—let your arms float about at your sides. If you lose your balance try to wobble slowly, and it will look like part of the walk. The feeling is up, down, up, down, gently floating.

Look at homework.

Have each person practice a short improvisation about landing on the moon, and then perform it.

Homework Assignment: Bring in a sketch that includes pelvic impulses.

114

1.

2.

3.

4.

Inclinations; rotations; reverse inclinations and rotations; combinations in
two directions and falling into their final
positions; four walks with a high knee;
walking on a tightrope; merry-go-round;
rowing.

Do the inclinations and rotations.

Reverse Inclinations and Rotations: By the time you reach Lesson Twenty-Six,
you should be proficient at doing the inclinations and rotations. The positions
should be clear and precise by now. The reverse inclinations start from the
other end, and should not be tried until you have mastered the regular way.
Forward: Start in the double-zero position. Relax the pelvis, and incline the
pelvis forward, keeping the rest of the body in line with it, so you are bent
forward as when you did each part separately. Now incline the waist forward as
far as it will go, keeping the head, neck, and chest in line with it. Now incline
the chest forward, keeping the head and neck in line with it. Incline the neck
forward, keeping the head in line with it, and finally incline the head forward as
far as it will go. You should now be fully inclined forward.
Coming up is harder: Lift the head, but only until it is in line with the neck; lift
the neck (keeping the head in line with it) until it is in line with the chest; lift
the chest (keeping the head and neck in line with it) until it is in line with the
waist; lift the waist (keeping all above it in line with it) until it is in line with the
pelvis. You should now be in the position you were in when you made the first
move and inclined the pelvis forward—bring the pelvis and all in line with it to
upright. You are now back in the double-zero position. Do it several times.
Side: Start in the double-zero position. Incline the pelvis to the right, bending
the left knee, and keeping the rest of the body in line with the pelvis. Now
incline the waist to the right, keeping the head, neck, and chest in line with it;
incline the chest to the right, keeping the head and neck in line with it; incline
the neck to the right, keeping the head in line with it; incline the head to the
right. You should now be fully inclined to the right. Come up by first bringing
the head in line with the neck; then bring the head and neck in line with the
chest, then bring the head, neck, and chest in line with the waist; then lift the
waist so that it and all above it are in line with the pelvis, and then staying in
line, put the left heel down, and straighten the body up into the double-zero
position. Do it to the left, and repeat it a few times. Whenever you come up,
have the feeling of extending the body longer as you bring the next piece in line.
Rear: Same principle—Right foot forward, as for a rear inclination. Incline just
the pelvis to the rear, bending the back knee, and keeping the body in line with
the right leg. Now incline the waist to the rear, with the rest in line with it.
Incline the chest to the rear, with the head and neck staying in line with it;
incline the neck to the rear, and then the head. You are now fully inclined to
the rear.

Come back—lift the head until it is in line with the neck; lift the neck until it and the head are in line with the chest, lift the chest until they are all in line with the waist; lift the waist, and everything should be in line with the pelvis; lift the pelvis by straightening the left leg. You should be upright again. Try it a few times.

Do the combinations involving two directions—Lesson Twelve—and when you get the final position of each one, straighten up and then try to fall back into the final position. Try to extend each part as far as you did when you went through all the steps to get there. Do it a couple of times on each final position. Practice the four walks with a high knee—Lessons Nine and Twenty-three.

Walking on a Tightrope: Picture a tightrope. Step out onto it, with your arms out to the sides and your knees bent a bit. It has a little give in it, which makes you bounce up and down a bit as you walk on it. Keep this bounce—very slight when you're not walking, a bit bigger as you step. If you jump, bounce high, and then less and less until it settles down to a very slight give in the imaginary rope. There are two wobbles you can use: One is from the waist up, and your arms go up and down as the chest tilts from side to side; the other is from the waist down—the pelvis and knees—and on this one the arms remain level, and the upper body does not move as you move the pelvis from side to side. Try walking on the rope, alternating the wobbles, keeping the knees bent so that you can continue the slight up and down movement caused by the rope giving a little. Work out your own combinations and story. Try tricks or whatever you want after you can do it keeping the up and down and side-to-side at the same time.

Practice the merry-go-round—Lesson Twenty-one.

Practice rowing a boat—Lesson Twenty-one.

Look at the homework.

If there is time, have each one do a short improvisation using some of the things done in class today.

Homework Assignment: Bring in a sketch which includes two illusions (walks, climbs, pushes or pulls, the several we did today, etc.).

LESSON TWENTY-SEVEN

The body as a unit; beginning and advanced hand exercises; balance exercises with forward, side, and rear inclinations; comic walks; duos.

Do the exercises with the body as a unit—Lesson Five.
Do the hand exercises—beginning, Lesson Three, and advanced, Lesson Eleven.
Do the balance exercises—Lessons Twelve and Nineteen.
Practice the comic walks—Lesson Twelve.
Do the duos described in Lesson Fourteen.
Look at homework.

Homework Assignment: Bring in a sketch in which the body is kept as a unit.

Inclinations; rotations; reverse inclinations and rotations; transtations; tug-of-war; advanced rope-pulling; merry-go-round; walking on a tightrope; walking on the moon; paddling a canoe; walking with a cane; walking with crutches; limping; riding a bicycle; facial exercises; improvisations.

Do the inclinations and rotations.
Do the reverse inclinations and rotations—Lesson Twenty-six.
Do the transtations.
Practice the tug-of-war—Lesson Two.
Practice advanced rope-pulling—Lesson Sixteen.
Practice the merry-go-round—Lesson Twenty-one.
Practice walking on a tightrope—Lesson Twenty-six.
Practice walking on the moon—Lesson Twenty-five.

Paddling a Canoe: If you can, try to see the film on the Peking Opera that is in most school libraries. There is a mime sequence in it that is superb in which a man poles and paddles a boat with a woman at the other end.
Bend your knees, and practice sliding across the floor by lifting both heels, moving them to the left, and then lifting the balls of both feet and sliding them to the left. Keep the body from the waist up rotated to the left, and try to become smooth and fast as you slide. Hold the imaginary paddle with your left hand on the top and your right down on it. As you dip it into the water and pull back, increase the speed of your slide; as you lift the paddle out of the water, slow your sliding gradually. Try to give the rhythm that would occur if a boat were actually being paddled in water. Your body is rotated to the left so that it faces the direction in which you are going. You can lift the paddle out of the water and dip it in on the left side of the boat for a few strokes, but keep your direction fairly constant. Try doing maneuvers in the water, turning the boat, etc. Practice.

Walking with a Cane: The secret of this illusion is to place the point of the cane on the floor in front of you, with the cane vertical, and then catch up to the cane as you walk towards it. When you reach it, place it forward again, and then catch up to it. Your elbow must bend enough to keep the cane's height the same. It will shrink if you don't bend the elbow enough. If you are young, you may catch up to the cane in one step, if you are old, it may take four steps. But always place the cane, keep it in place, and walk to it.

Walking with Crutches: Put the imaginary crutches under your arms, with the crutches at an angle, so that the points are in front of you on the floor; your arms are in front of you with the elbows straight. Keeping both knees straight, step up onto the half-toe of the right foot as you lift both shoulders to give the impression of the crutches pushing up, and bring the arms in close to the sides, and continue the step forward landing on the flat of the left foot. Then swing the crutches out to the side a bit as you bring them forward again, and at the same time point the right foot forward. It is as if the right leg is part of the crutch, and rising up on the half-toe should give the impression of rising up on the crutches. The lift of the shoulders gives the impression that something is pushing them up, and that there is weight on them. Practice this on each leg, and then try one crutch: The principle is the same.

Walk With Crutches

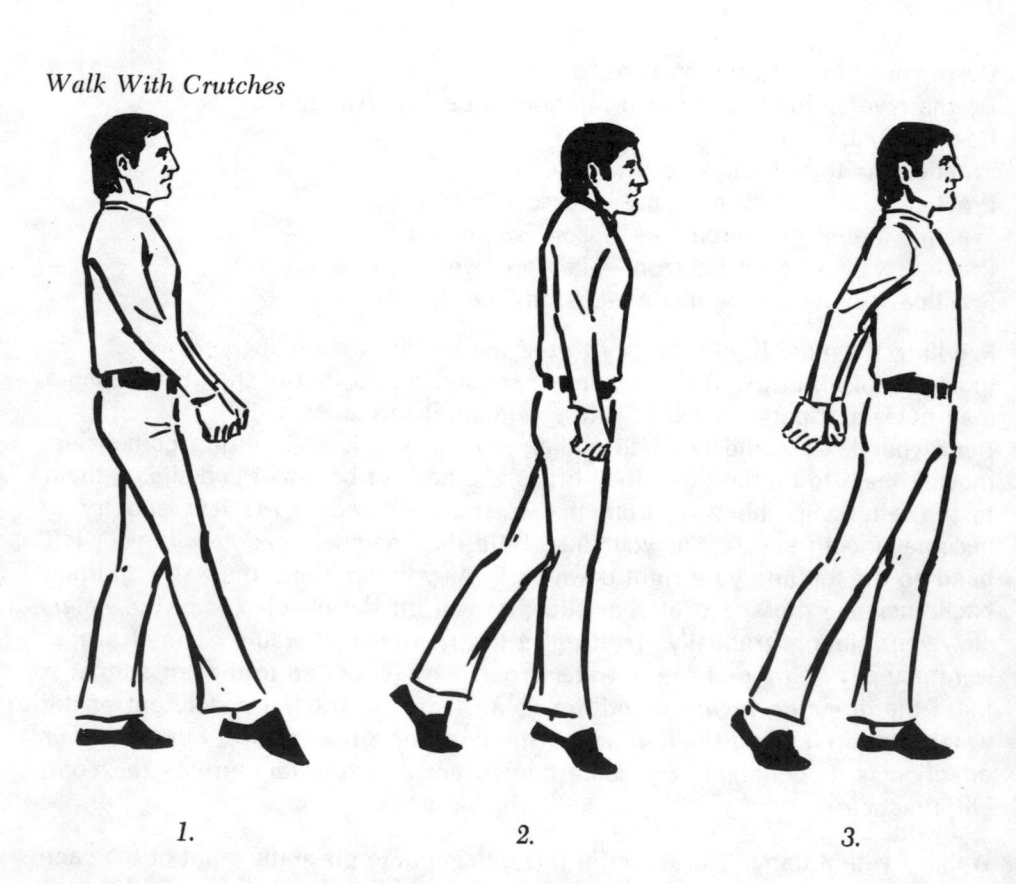

1.   2.   3.

Limping: There are several basic limps: The most common one is the painful-foot limp—this can be from an injury, thorn, etc. Just keep the hurt foot on the ground as short a time as possible. Try to feel the pain, and get off it quick, so that the good foot takes the weight. Try the straight-knee limp—walk with a straight knee in one leg, but use the other one normally. Try the pelvic-thrust limp: The injured leg needs impetus from the pelvis to throw it forward—lead with the pelvis, letting the leg lag behind, and thrust forward, letting the impulse travel down the leg, propelling it forward. Step normally with the other foot. Try each leg, and try various severities of injury.

Riding a Bicycle: There are several ways to do this illusion, and first everyone should try to figure out his own. Everyone should be sure, however, to keep the handle bars steady. You can do a variation of the illusory walk, you can move around the room in a kind of prancing run, or others.

My favorite way is to do it in place: Stand on the left leg with the knee bent and grasp the handle bars, keeping the back very slightly bent forward. The right leg is in the air in front of you, with the knee slightly bent. As you pull the right leg in, straightening the knee, in a regular bicycle motion, go to the half-toe of the left foot; as the right is under you and coming up around again, put the left heel down, as the right continues around again, and is pulling in again, go up on the left half-toe again, and then put the heel down as the right is under you again. Continue. Keep the handle bars still and level, and after you're going smoothly, look around at the scenery as you ride.

121

Riding a Bicycle

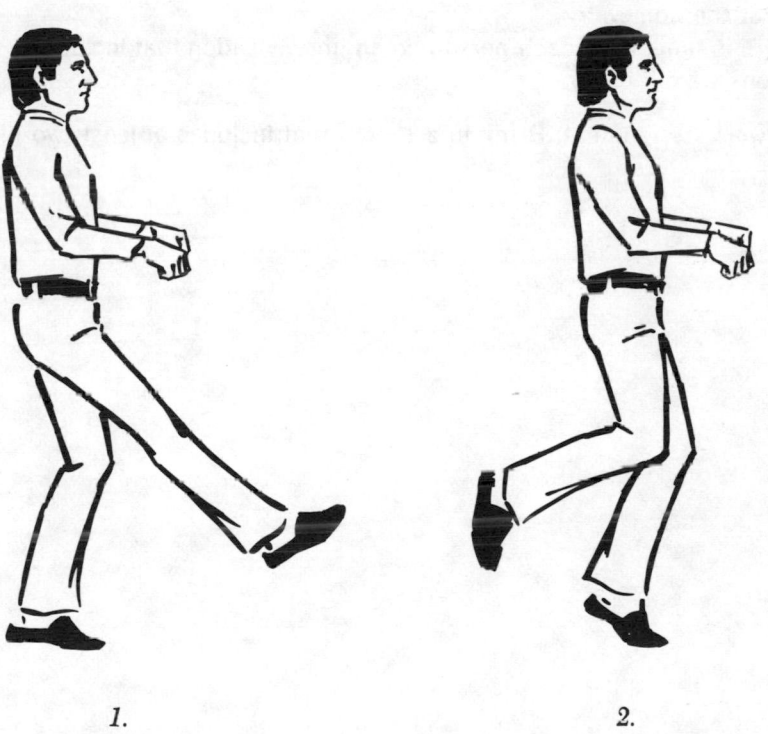

1.   2.

Facial Expressions: Do the exercises we did in Lessons One and Two, including the five expressions we did. Here are a few more: Afraid—let the mouth hang open a little, open the eyes as far as possible without lifting the eyebrows. Wonder—pucker the mouth as if saying "Ooooooh," and lift the eyebrows high with the eyes wide open. Fiendish—a big grin, with the eyebrows down. There is one you can try that is used in all Spanish and Italian movies: it means "I love you," "I hate you," "Go away," "Come back," "You've returned," "you've gone," and "I have to sneeze." It's called General Emotion (never use it except in stark melodrama)—lift the eyebrows, let the eyes droop, and pull the corners of the mouth down with the mouth very slightly open. It varies depending whether you put the fist on the chest, the back of the hand on the forehead, or the finger under the nose.

Please bear in mind that all the expressions are only exercises to stretch the face, and are not the visualization of emotions, even though we give them names. When you want to show an emotion, feel it, and only show what really happens. What happens will be a little bigger as a result of these exercises.

Look at the homework.

If there is time, have each person do an improvisation that includes some of the illusions we did today.

Homework Assignment: Bring in a sketch that includes at least two illusions.

Inclinations; rotations; reverse inclinations and rotations; transtations; putting on gloves; opening doors; lighting
a cigarette; chopping with an axe; bell-
ringing; sawing; looking; playing two
characters; object transformations.

123

Do the inclinations and rotations.
Do the reverse inclinations and rotations—Lesson Twenty-six.
Do the transtations.

Putting on Gloves: Bring all the fingers together—be sure they are all inside your imaginary glove, and work them into the fingers of the glove. The thumb will tend to be left outside. If you are proficient at the advanced hand wriggle, here is a place you can use it: Wriggle your fingers into the glove. When the fingers are in, pull the glove at the wrist, and at the same time, straighten the fingers.

Opening Doors: Be sure the knob stays level with the floor, and moves in an arc as the door opens. Practice opening doors in all directions, and with both hands. Try a swinging door and a French door. Be sure you let go of the knob, and that you don't squash the knob.

Lighting a Cigarette: Be sure you leave a little hole between your lips for the cigarette, and be sure you let go of it with your fingers when you place it between your lips. Be sure the space between your fingers is of cigarette thickness and not of cigar thickness. When you light it, strike the match, and then tremble your hand that holds the match to signify the flickering of the flame, and stop the tremble when you blow it out.

Chopping with an Axe: Stand with your feet apart, with the imaginary axe over your shoulder, and your hands about eighteen inches apart, as they would be on the handle of a real axe. Lead with your pelvis as you swing the axe forward, then the chest, and just before the axe strikes, bring the top hand down next to the lower one, so they are together on the impact. Now, using a chest impulse, pull back sharply on the axe handle to dislodge it from the wood. Then, as you swing it back over your shoulder, slide the upper hand up the handle, so the hands are back in the starting position again apart. The dislodging move is important to the illusion: Make it clear.

Bell-Ringing: Etienne Decroux seemed to think this exercise was important, and had his students do it over and over again for days. Perhaps he was influenced by the presence of Notre Dame Cathedral so near him. Reach over your head to the right, and take hold of an imaginary bell-cord, and lift the left knee into the

1.   *2.*

air at your side. Transtation your chest down and to the left as you pull your arms down and to the left as if pulling the cord, step onto the left foot, keeping the knee bent, and lift the right knee into the air at your side. As you swing the arms up and to the right, transtation the chest to the right and up, step onto the right foot, and as you straighten the right knee as the arms reach their maximum height, lift the left leg into the air at your side. Try it several times on both sides.

Sawing: Place your left hand on the thing-to-be-sawn, and grasp the handle of the saw in your right (if you're left handed, yes, you may do the opposite). Use chest impulses, with a rotation of the chest to the right as you pull back and to the left as you push the saw forward.

Looking: There is a classic position for looking off into the distance. Flatten your hand, with the fingers curved slightly upward, and place it in the air about a foot in front of your head and about six inches higher than your head. Try to make right angles with the rest of the arm, so that the upper arm is parallel to the ground, and the forearm as perpendicular as possible. The knuckles will tend to bend—don't let them. Now just raise the eyebrows and gaze off. Try it on the other side.

Playing Two Characters: The trick is in the transition: You may use either a turn or a jump to change characters, and while turning or jumping, you must be neither character—the jump is separate. The first times you do these, if you are for instance facing stage right as the hero, turn to your right, so that your back is to the audience on the turn as you change to the villain. Land, facing stage left, become the villain, and then act as the villain. When you want to go back to being the hero, turn to the left (back to audience again), land, facing stage right, become the hero, and act as the hero. If the characters are far apart, leap to the spot instead of turning. When you become adept, you may do the turn the other way, so that it is towards the audience.

Have each person practice playing two characters in a short improvisation, and perform them.

Look at homework.

If there is any time left, do object transformations—Lesson Twenty.

125

Homework Assignment: Bring in a sketch in which you play two characters with contrasting emotions.

Inclinations; rotations; combinations involving three directions, and falling into their final positions; level hand; beginning and advanced hand exercises; leans; walks #1 and #2, illusory walks #1 and #2, improvisations.

126

Do the inclinations and rotations.
Do the combinations of inclinations and rotations involving two directions—Lesson Two—and practice falling into the final positions—Lesson Twenty-six. Now do the combinations involving three directions—Lesson Thirteen—and practice falling into these final positions. Be sure you extend each position to its maximum.
Do the beginning and advanced hand exercises.

The Level Hand: Practice holding the hand level with the thumb in against the side of the hand, the fingers extended and touching. Try to get it absolutely boardlike, with no bends in any of the knuckles. Try bending the wrist without breaking the line of the hand, and turning the wrist without breaking. This has no immediate application, but is a further control that you should have.

Leans: To give the impression of leaning far to one side against an imaginary object, such as a bar or a wall, you must have equal proportions of your weight on each side of your center of gravity. Stand with your weight on your left foot, lean way out to the right, putting your elbow on an imaginary bar with your wrist dangling (you can transtation the chest to the right, too); cross your right foot in front of the left, reach it to the left, and put the toe on the floor. The balance is maintained by the position of the right leg. The audience will be watching the chest and arm, and won't realize that the balance is being kept only because the right leg has crossed to the left side of the center of gravity, balancing the lean to the right by the upper body. Do the same lean against an imaginary wall, with your hand flat against it. Try the other side. Try leaning while sitting. If you prop an elbow, let your wrist dangle a moment, and then settle—it helps give the impression that your elbow is resting on something solid.

Do walk #1—Lesson One.
Do walk #2—Lesson Eleven.
Do illusory walk #1—Lesson Four—and illusory walk #2—Lesson Nine.
Look at the homework.
Do some duets—Lesson Four.
This is the end of the sequence, and if a final project is to be brought in, it should be a four or five minute sketch created by the performer, that is practiced enough to be performable, and in which all illusions needed to tell the story are done clearly and well.

Leans

1.   2.

TEACHING PLAN

The preceding lessons are the first year's work in mime, and if there is one class a week, it can be followed as written for thirty weeks. The first ten lessons are a kind of introduction to the technique, and include several of the special things that we only do once, or occasionally. The next ten lessons go more deeply into the work with the body and the hands, with a few more illusions, and the last ten weeks deal more with the illusions and uses of the technique, as well as going into more advanced body work.

If there are two lessons a week, and the class is more than a dozen people, you can do the technique on the first day and perform the assignments and do improvisations on the second day. If the class is small, four or six people, I would suggest doing the same class twice each week: The repetition won't hurt. The second time you can do the exercises faster, and so have more time to do extra improvisations. If a special exercise is being done, like using a minimum of effort or the exercise on hunger and appetite, only do them once the week they are done, and perhaps move on to the next technique class. If you have extra time in a class, you can always do duets or a slow-motion exercise to finish out the time.

When practicing the inclinations, I would suggest doing each one about three times, and then move on to the next one. Don't try to learn it all at once; or as my old Karate teacher said: "Make haste slowly." The effect of the exercises is cumulative: it will gradually sink in. Do the combinations once in each direction when you come to them, do the balance turns three or four times to each side. Repeat the pelvic exercises four or so times on each side, etc. Don't dwell on each little move too long or you'll end up doing only one or two exercises in a class. The time to dwell is when practicing outside of class. Then you can perfect each little movement. No one can learn the illusory walks by doing them for five minutes in a class, so practice will be necessary, but that is up to the individual. Always work for being big and clear and simple. Do each exercise slowly and right—later it can get faster. Try to stay in sequence as much as possible, without jumping ahead to future lessons, unless you have a particular need for some specific illusion. But don't try the reverse inclinations or the combinations until you have perfected the simple inclinations and rotations.

To create a mime sketch, use the formula given in the homework assignments: Start with an object, a place, or a character, improvise, and keep the best ones and develop them. If you use narration with the mime, try to have the physical action be either an extension-development of the words, or for the action to be different from the words, so that the audience gets its message from the combination. I like to use live music with all performances, but that is up to you. Good luck.

CLASSIC MIME MAKEUP

The white classic makeup probably dates from the time of the Romans, when the mimes would put flour on their faces, and darken the eyes and mouths, so that they could be seen from a distance. The principle is that since the projection of the facial image is so important, you emphasise the features by outlining the eyes and darkening the mouth. I stopped using the makeup in 1965. It takes thirty to forty minutes to put it on and fifteen to take it off. It's messy, it drips on your costume when you sweat, and I prefer not to be an image, but to be a person. However, I'm sure that some of you would like to be in the tradition, so I'll tell you how to put it on and how to take it off.

You start with clown white, and experience has shown me that Stein's works the best. The secret is in the white. If it is on too thin you see the skin through it, and if it's too thick it gets globby. So it takes practice. Put it on thick enough to cover so that nothing shows through, and smooth it so there are no streaks. Cover the area that a mask would cover: don't put any on the ears or up into the hairline or on the neck, just the face itself. The line at the top should be definite, as should the line in front of the ears and at the chin and jawline. You can pick the shape that fits your own face, or even make a design with the outer border.

Next is the powder. Don't use talcum powder it leaves the face tacky and untouchable. Use cornstarch: It leaves the makeup so dry that you can touch your face as if it were skin when the makeup is finished. Have a big powder puff, lean forward over a sink or over a newspaper, pour a large pile of cornstarch on the puff, and pat it on to the face. Only pat as long as there's cornstarch on the puff, then pour plenty more onto it, and pat some more, until you've hit the entire mask. You can touch your face gently with your finger tips to find spots you've missed, but cornstarch is cheap, so pat on plenty before you touch. Once the makeup is set with the cornstarch, you can't change it without taking the whole thing off.

When you've powdered the whole mask, keep patting and then pressing with the puff, and then, when you've no sticky places left, lightly brush the excess off with your fingertips. Take a Kleenex and dust off your eyelashes. Hopefully you didn't get any of the clown white on your lashes, so the cornstarch won't stick. Now wet a piece of Kleenex and wipe the excess off around the edge of the mask. The makeup won't smear now even if you wet the edge of it. Now your face is all white.

Next come the black lines. The best liner is Max Factor black liquid eye-liner. All the others, Elizabeth Arden, Revlon, and the rest tend to crack when you use them over clown white, but the Max Factor one has an oil base, and goes on and stays on the best. Draw (with a brush) a thin line around your eyes; use your own shape: not like the exaggerated makeup of ballet—just outline your own eye. Get as close to your lashes as you can comfortably. Use the brush and lightly blacken your lashes. Use the end of a bobby pin, or a key, or a piece of wood, and draw the shape of eyebrow you want on your forehead. It should be slightly higher than your own eyebrows, and can be any shape you want: They can slant up or down or be curved—find a way that you like. Now dig the makeup out of the eyebrow pattern, so the skin shows. Fill it in with the black liner. The eyebrows are raised so they can be seen better from a distance. Next, if you wish, draw a black line around the outside of your mask. This line is optional. I use it, Marceau uses part of it, and others don't use it at all. You can shape it as you wish, if you use it. The only other lines you should use might be dashes either out from the side of the eyes (Marceau uses these) or points under the eyes (I use this, and don't like it when anyone else does). Then, if you are a man, outline your own lipline with a thin black line, but women shouldn't do this. Now use red lipstick—women just follow your own lipline, men fill in the outlined lips.

Mime makeup is not exaggerated like clown makeup, and only uses these three colors: red, white and black. You never use blue or green eyeliner or any other color, and you don't exaggerate the shape of your features. The only thing you might add to the above makeup might be a round spot of red on each cheek for women; but this is optional, and might not be right for certain characters. There used to be a girl in my troupe who put a red heart on each cheek. This makeup takes many applications before you get it smooth, but gradually it becomes sharp and clearer as you practice.

To get it off: The best solvent for the makeup is a thin oil. We use salad oil, but you can use baby oil, mineral oil, cold cream, or anything else you want. Salad oil works the best. Pour a little into your hand, and rub it into the face. Don't go near the eyes the first time, but do the rest, rubbing to dissolve the makeup. Wipe it off with Kleenex. Oil the face again, getting closer to the eyes, and wipe it off again. The third oiling, you can go right up to the lashes, rub the oil in all over the face again, and then wipe it off. Three oilings should just about do it. Then wash you face with Dial soap (or any other one with hexachloraphene in it), dry it, and wash it and dry it again. It should be pretty clean by now. Be sure you get it all off, and it won't bother your skin.

So there you have it—just in case you want to use it.

A BRIEF HISTORY OF ME

Actually I could write several completely different autobiographies, and they'd all be true: they'd each follow different simultaneous lines of my life. One, of course, would be my life in the theatre; another might be about my spiritual life—"From Jew-Atheist to Religious-Mystic"; another might be about politics —"How to go from Pinko to Puritan Without Losing your Humanitarian Ethic"; another might be a series of romantic adventures, like Frank Harris' autobiography, ending with the last chapter, "From Profligate to Husband-Who-Doesn't-Mess-Around"; perhaps another might be "From Bohemian to Artist in Twenty Slow Years." In this short version we'll stick to the theatre, although if I hadn't gone through a spiritual change I probably would never have become a real artist, and if I hadn't been after romantic adventure I never would have entered the theatre in the first place. In time, of course, motives changes.

I was born in New York City, April 24, 1929, at 1:00 P.M., with a different first name. My first appearance on a stage was in kindergarten in Brooklyn, where I played a duck. Yes, I loved it, but who doesn't at that age. It was, of course, in pantomime, and perhaps the real theatre historians among you will include this in your research as a "significant influence." I decided at the age of nine or so to be a chemist when I grew up, and with my father's help set up a laboratory in the basement. After a few months of experimenting, I put on a show of chemical magic for the kids on the block, charging them a nickel each. See the trend? I didn't until much later. In junior high school I was in a play about James Audubon, and had a small part: one scene with a few lines. As I was about to go on stage I saw a vase of daffodils in the wings and grabbed one. I entered with my nose in the yellow daffodil, took it out to speak, and then put it back and sniffed. The audience roared every time I did it, and gave me a big hand as I exited, and just as big a response on the curtain call when I entered with the flower again. As you can see, I've never forgotten it. Meanwhile my aspirations had changed a bit, and I was now convinced that being a doctor was the only life to live. I did join the cheerleaders in high school though, because I liked to jump around. (Ah, ha!)

When I started college at Emory University in Atlanta, Georgia, I was studying pre-med, but I immediately joined The Emory Players, appeared in several of their productions, and was even farmed out to a girls' school to play the leading man in one of their plays. But I never thought the theatre was something you'd make your life's work, so when I realized medicine was not for me, I switched to pre-law. Meanwhile, I had embarked into political activity (I ran an inter-racial dance in Atlanta in 1948), started romantic adventures, and got involved with football parlay cards—but those stories are for another book.

At nineteen I switched to Adelphi University in Long Island, New York, still studying pre-law. When I registered there I noticed that you could take modern dance instead of Physical Education, so I signed up for it. I had had a friend in Atlanta who used to leap around the living room at parties, and the girls were always interested in him; also I was always attracted to girls who were dancers. So I started dancing with Maxine Munt and Al Brooks, and before long was studying dance every night in New York at The New Dance Group, later joined the Hindu-Javanese-Balinese-etc. dance group of a marvelous dancer named

Hadassah, and studied Haitian dance with Jean Leon Destine, and still later studied with Martha Graham. I switched my major to theatre.

At Adelphi I met Phillip Schrager, a student who had come back to college to finish his degree. He had worked with Jean-Louis Barrault and Louis Jouvet in Paris, and had been a student and then a faculty member at The Dramatic Workshop in New York. Phil began to teach me acting, and directed me in a couple of plays. Part of his teaching included mime.

After college I got an apartment in Manhattan, and when Phil split up with his wife he moved onto my living-room couch. I studied acting with Morris Carnovsky, and continued with dance. I took a job in an office after college, lasted three months, quit, and didn't work at a job again until I was 37. In December 1951 I got a bad case of laryngitis that lasted two months. In January '52 I said to Phil, "Let's do a show in pantomime." He said "Okay," and we went into rehearsal. I booked us into The Circle-In-The-Square in the Village for two weekends, and in April 1952 we did the first ensemble mime performance in this country—A. A. Milne's poetry for children.

There were three girls in our group, which we called "The Mime Theatre"—I played all the male parts, and Phil did the narration. During the rehearsal period we were joined by a mad Frenchwoman who was a brilliant mime, Tchouky Mattei, and she helped with the technical direction. The show went well, and I was hooked.

Phil moved out shortly thereafter, and I started to study mime technique with Alvin Epstein, who had been the leading member of Etienne Decroux' company in Paris. Phil gave me the inspiration—Alvin showed me the real technique. That summer I started my own company; we did three hours of work every night: an hour of dance, an hour of acting, and an hour of mime. I taught them the mime that Alvin had taught me the week before; if I missed a class with Alvin, we had review. By the end of the summer we had enough material to do a show, and I booked Carnegie Recital Hall (the little hall—three hundred seats) for three performances. We called the group "The Pantomime Art Theatre," and I kept that name for four years. The show was in November 1952. We found that we needed time to change costumes between numbers, so four folk singers I knew did a number or two twice during the program. This was the first stage appearance of Mary Travers, who later became part of Peter, Paul and Mary. We were not a spectacular success. Brooks Atkinson was in the audience, and thank goodness he didn't write a review. The mime was crude, the audience was tiny, and I found out how much I had to learn. I didn't do another performance for two years. During this time I taught mime, practiced the technique, and developed material.

We started doing shows again, a new one every month, at the old Malin Studios on West 46th Street, mostly based on improvisations that were done in class. Some of the people in the troupe at about this time were Leo Rauch, who is now a philosophy professor at New York University, Diana Sands, the actress, Louis Nirenberg, of New York University, a mathematician, Michael and Eileen Mislove, Selma Marcus, Belle Hara, who was my old lady, and was very beautiful and very talented, Muriel Livingston, Tony Montanaro, Lila Lewis, Sheila Hellman, Bobbie Chifos, Sheila La Farge, Chris Frangos, Angelo Laiacona, Bob Collins, Lily Abouaf; and some of our accompanists were Ramblin' Jack Elliot, Dick Rosmini, Ray Boguslav. We always had live music, usually guitar, and sometimes 'cello and recorder or flute, and some of the pieces had narration.

We ended this period with another shot at Carnegie Recital Hall, and did George Haimsohn's version of **Hamlet** as one of the pieces. It told the entire plot in twenty minutes, and was hilarious. Jack Elliot sat on the apron with his feet dangling into the audience and drawled the narration as he played his guitar. We won the annual Showbusiness Award for 1955.

In August 1955 Marcel Marceau came to New York, and visited my studio on Sixth Avenue, where we did a special performance for him. He invited me to come and work with him in Paris the following spring, and I said I'd be there. I had applied for a Fulbright Scholarship the previous year, had been granted it, after passing all tests, and then denied it by the State Department. I assume it was because I had been somewhat subversive in my late teens (like the inter-racial dance I ran in Atlanta) and this was right after the McCarthy era. But Marceau's success opened doors for us that had been closed before: we had auditioned for television before, and never been hired. Now TV was interested in mime, and we started to work occasionally.

At that time I was living in a small basement apartment on West 81st Street, full of books, paintings, props, second-hand furniture; the bedroom was in the kitchen, and I had my sandal workshop in the bathroom, where I could sit on the toilet and make sandals. There were four of us staying there at that time— Sykes Equen, who later became my first wife, George Hopkins, the comedian, and a dancer named Judith, and a fifth, Terry McGuire, who kept his things in a neat pile in the living room. It was so crowded I had to get out. I saw an ad for a loft on Second Avenue and Eighth Street, and with a borrowed twenty five dollars, made a down payment, and then raised several hundred dollars from friends, and opened the Pantomime Art Theatre. We built dressing rooms, wings, had a raised stage, put in a kitchen, and built a large apartment at the end, with a living room and a bedroom. We disguised the bedroom wall so that it seemingly had no door, so that when the building inspectors came they wouldn't know anyone was living there. The living room was officially the theatre lounge. Malcomb Newman, the artist, was the stage manager, and we all helped build. We opened a mime show, and every Friday night had a Dixie-land Jazz party after the show, at midnight; and Ted Joans and I ran the Mau-Mau ball there a couple of times. As the weather got colder, lots of people we knew who lived in chilly apartments came to sleep in the theatre. Sykes kind of ran the place, and performed with the group, George moved out after building one shaky wall, and Judith ran off with a director who used to sleep on our living room couch. After the mime show, we booked in a series of plays; the final one of the year won the "Obie" for the best original drama of 1956.

January 1956 I appeared on a television show, which gave me enough for fare to Europe, and that spring I went to Paris. Sykes stayed in New York to mind the theatre. Marceau was preparing a show when I arrived, so I found Decroux, and took class with him every day. It didn't matter that I understood little French, because Decroux repeated everything so many times that I couldn't help but understand. There were two kinds of students in Decroux' classes: disciples and sceptics. I, of course, fell in the latter category, but I went along with whatever he gave us, because I really wanted to know what he had to say. He is a brilliant, but tedious teacher. Marceau opened his show, and I went many nights, and worked out with him on the stage of his theatre a few times. I would say that the main thing that I learned in my three months in Europe was to keep going in the direction I was headed—it was okay.

When I was going to return home I told Decroux I would only be attending one more class, and he said, "Next time you come, show us some of this, uh, pantomime you say you do." I said, "Okay," and practiced a short improvisation in which I did the illusory walk, saw something, stopped, looked both ways, stepped over a little fence, picked a flower, smelled it, saw someone coming, jumped back over the fence, and did the illusory run. When I finished showing this to Decroux, I expected him to be either smiling, or critical, or something. His face was bright red, and he screamed at me, "Where did you get that walk?!?" I said, "You mean this?" and did the illusory walk. He yelled, "Yes that walk!" I said, "I saw Barrault do it in **Children of Paradise,** and Alvin Epstein worked on it with me in New York." He screamed, "I invented that walk in 1934. You're all alike, the three of you—you think you know everything—you and Barrault and Marceau. None of you do it right. Barrault does it like **this,**" and he proceeded to mimic Barrault, "Marceau does it like a clown, with his head waving," and he did an exaggerated version of Marceau's walk, "and you can't do it either. Three know-it-alls." I thanked him for putting me in such good company, thanked him for all I had learned from him, and left.

Meanwhile, the building department had closed our theatre in New York, and when I got back Sykes and I got married, and went to Los Angeles. An actor named Richard Gilden and I opened The Theatre Workshop after I had been in Hollywood for some months, and I taught mime and acting, and we had a costume party every two weeks to raise the rent. Then I ran the Beverly Hills playhouse for Brian Hutton, and put on a season of plays, including one by Aldous Huxley, who came every night to see it. I directed some plays, including O'Neill's **The Hairy Ape,** and started performing mime in a coffee-shop, The Unicorn, on Sunset Strip. After several months we moved to The Cabaret Concertheatre, ran a couple of months, and then performed at The Club Renaissance on the Strip. My guitarist-narrator was Fred Engelberg, who began to write pieces for me. Sykes and I split up, and the leading lady in the troupe was Louise Sorell, who became a fine actress. Elliot Fayad was with us, and Larry Breitman, and then Ziva Rodann, an Israeli actress who had done mime in Israel with Shai K. Ophir replaced Louise. In April 1959, Fred, Louise, and I went to San Francisco, to the Hungry i, and called the act "The Mime and Me." All the California newspaper reviewers gave us rave reviews.

During this time I appeared on several of the running television shows as an actor, and was always teaching mime somewhere. I studied film direction with Ted Post, and learned much from him and from the guest lecturers he brought in.

Work in California got slack, and since I still considered myself a New Yorker, I returned home. I had been doing a lot of painting towards the end of 1959, so that summer I rented an artist's loft on 14th Street, intending to do a lot of great paintings. In California I had been doing abstract expressionistic paintings by laying a piece of masonite or wood on the floor and schmearing. Some of them were quite good, and I figured that in a real studio I couldn't miss. Every painting I did that summer stank, and I threw them all away.

When I drove across country that May 1959, something happened that I feel is significant. Somewhere in the middle of the country, after driving for about a day and a half, alternating driving time with a friend, we stopped to eat, and I found that I could hit a pole with a rock twenty times out of twenty from fifty feet away. I don't know what caused it, but I suddenly remembered the title of a

book I had seen in the Unicorn bookshop, called **Zen and the Art of Archery.**
When I had seen the book on a shelf, I had remarked to a friend, "Isn't that a
silly title—what could archery possibly have to do with some Oriental philosophy?" I suddenly knew what that book was about. And I felt that I had
reached some kind of a turning point in my life. I threw some more rocks at the
pole, and never missed.

That summer Fred Engelberg and I auditioned our act at The Blue Angel in
New York, and the owner watched for about a minute, and then began to talk
to the man he was sitting with, and didn't look at us again. Fred and I worked
in the mountains a couple of times, and we appeared on The Today Show, with
Marilyn Gennaro as the girl in the group. Fred went back to California at the end
of the summer, and I started to formulate plans for a mime show. That fall I
found a backer, Brinley Maury, and shot my first film, a fourteen-minute photo-
graphic essay on a fourteen year old girl called "Afternoon of a Faunette,"
which subsequently won a small award in a festival. The girl was Cary Karmel,
and she later performed with the mime troupe.

I started casting for the mime show I wanted to do as the fall ended. I was
sharing a two room apartment six flights up on MacDougal Street with Stanley
Wagner and five other people. We slept on mattresses on the floor, bundled to
keep warm, and all had bright hopes. I cast Willy Switkes, who had worked with
me before, Martha Howell, who was precise, and then found Lucienne Bridou in
a health food restaurant—she was beautiful, and became our leading lady, and
Rusdi Lane appeared after a year and a half with Marceau in Paris. Weston
Gavin, who had been like my little brother for about six years, filled in as the
guitarist-narrator (I expected Fred to return for the show when it was ready),
and we were ready to rehearse. I borrowed a studio in the Living Theatre from
the Becks, and we started working. On New Year's Eve I moved into my own
apartment on Morton Street; I had nothing but a double bed, two suitcases and
a box with my things, some paintings, and some pilfered wooden milk bottle
boxes to use as shelves. The gas and electricity weren't turned on yet, but it
felt great in candle-light to be alone and about to enter a New Year with
another shot at the brass ring.

The next afternoon Lucienne came to my new apartment to rehearse, and at
about six I walked her home. It was freezing out, so on the way we cut through
the back way of a coffee house that was then called The Commons to get warm
for a minute and to see what was happening. We passed a table, and I saw that
Stanley Wagner and Al, another of my former roommates, were starting to talk
to two tourist girls at a table. The girls were dressed all in black, with no lipstick, and lots of eye makeup, and had obviously come to look at beatniks. I
waved hello, rushed Lucienne home, and ran back. One of those girls was for
me. I went back to their table, smiled, kissed her on the side of the neck, and
we've been together ever since—over ten years as I write this, and four children. So January first is the anniversary we celebrate, although we were married
a few weeks later.

I found a producer for the show, Josh Miller, and we raised the eight thousand
dollars needed at three backers' auditions. My wedding was in a judge's office,
and after the ceremony we had lunch with my father, and went back to the
studio, where my wife, Hadria, painted helmets gold while I rehearsed. The
show, "The Mime and Me," opened at the Gramercy Arts Playhouse in April.
Fred never did make it, and Weston did the music; the stage managers were

Joanna Jones and Hamilton Camp. The show was well-rehearsed, the material was very strong, and the performance really felt good. We had an after-theatre supper with the producer and the backers, and Bill Heyer, who had directed for the final two weeks, so I could have an outside eye. We all expected a smash hit—this show was better than anything I had done in California.

Then the reviews came out. **The New York Times** had sent Lewis Funke, and he hated it, all except Weston. Walter Kerr on the Tribune was mixed, but at least he understood it. Funke, I believe, has the mind and sensitivity of a lead golf-ball, but he managed to condemn us with his short sentences and three letter words. By the time the good reviews in the **Post** and the **Telegram** came out the next day it was too late. To run in New York off-Broadway, you've got to get all good reviews, except in a very few cases. We received excellent reviews in **The Saturday Review, The Village Voice, Cue Magazine** and **The Villager,** but they are all weeklies, and by the time they came out we had run our two weeks, and were closed. For the last week, Hamilton filled in for Willy Switkes, who went into a Chekhov play. It was pretty dismal. No, not dismal, frustrating. More had gone into the show than the couple of months of rehearsal—eight years of doing mime had led up to it. We kept revising and improving up to the last performance.

I started teaching regularly at The Living Theatre, and that summer started doing "The Mime and Me" in coffee houses in the Village with Weston and Lucienne. We played at the Phase II for months, where you were paid by passing a basket at the end of the performance. I had my pregnant wife pass the basket, and we made enough to survive. And Weston, Sykes, and I performed in the mountains with Hadria working the lights; Sykes later married Weston's understudy. Later Weston and I did the act in The Bitter End, at The Village Gate, and did another show at The Provincetown Playhouse, and I directed a play by Jean Tardieux, the French theatre of the absurd playwrite. The Living Theatre did Pirandello's last play, **The Mountain Giants,** and I choreographed it, and then I appeared in their production of **Man is Man** as the Chinese priest for a short time. Weston and I did some commercials together, and I did some alone, and we appeared on The Today Show a lot, on Mike Wallace's "P.M.," and later I did "Celebrity Talent Scouts," with Chuck Morley as guitarist.

At about this time Julian and Judith Beck of the Living Theatre and I did a curious experiment together which was one of the forerunners of the kind of audience-involvement theatre they are doing today. Jackson MacLow had done a "theatre of chance" play called **The Marrying Maiden** at the Living Theatre, and we used his experiment as a basis for ours. The Becks were always interested in Artaud's concepts, and this was one of them.

We used the Phase II coffee house for our experiment. There were four readers in different parts of the room—Jackson, Julian, Judith, and another woman. There were four mimes—Cary Karmel, Gary Goodrow, Martha Howell, and I. We wore whiteface, and were positioned on the stage to begin with. The readers read Jackson's sentences, which were selected at random from various sources, especially the I-Ching. They timed the duration of each reading by throwing dice, and each had a watch to go by. So sometimes there would be one, sometimes two, sometimes all of them reading at once. The text was these short disjointed word-patterns. Near each reader was a stack of action-cards, with physical actions on them, such as: "hop around the room on one foot," "lie down and scream," "kiss someone," "clap your hands," and many more. The mimes were to improvise action either from what they heard from one of the readers who they happened to be near, or from one of the action cards, which they were to pick up after each improvised action was completed. The scenes were to take place either right there in the audience where we picked up the action-cards, or back on the stage, as we wished. The audience would see only the action that took place right near them, or they might see parts of other actions in other parts of the room. Most of the action took place among the tables of the audience, and the experiment was so successful that we did it four times.

In 1962 I formed a film company with Fred Baker; we both had features in mind we wanted to do, and decided to do some shorts first. We did five of them, and broke up the partnership. In June 1961, I had started doing a spiritual exercise called Subud. Weston had started it six months before me, and I saw profound changes in a short time, and decided to try it. At first I went because it made me high, but my motives soon changed as I began to experience a new kind of reality, and a new growing awareness in a new way. When the film company broke up, I had an office and a phone, and had met two musicians and a dancer in Subud. I felt it was time to open a theatre, and that if possible this strong spiritual force I was in contact with should be part of it. My wife and I had moved uptown to the West Side; she is tall and beautiful, and had tried high fashion modeling for a couple of months, and hated it, and had just become pregnant again. Konrad Kaufman, the drummer, Lucas Mason, trumpet player, and his wife, Paula, the dance teacher—choreographer at Bryn Mawr, and I started auditioning people for our new theatre. We found about fifteen people, a theatre and acting school on Third Avenue and Thirty-third Street became available just when we needed it, and we were given several thousand dollars to open the place, mostly from two backers, J. I. Rodale, and Dr. John Myers.

As we prepared to go into the theatre, we did a couple of performances of a new mime show called "Move Up!" at a concert hall on 57th Street, received good reviews, and, as 1963 started, we moved into The Noble Path Theatre. One of the cast members on 57th Street was Suzanne Fox, who later married a mime, Ken Martin, and performs with him now. Rosemary Heyer was the leading lady, and was singled out by reviewers.

At the Noble Path Theatre I ran classes in acting and mime, and we prepared to open a revised edition of "Move Up!" The cast included Linda Eskenas, Hallie Goodman, Annemarie Polonyi, Jerry Santini (who had been trained by Paul Curtis), David Cole, and Peter McGee. Paula Mason was a central figure, and Konrad played about forty percussive instruments, Lucas played many flutes as well as trumpet, and Michael Lobel joined us on guitar, bass, and flute. We based the program titles on the I-Ching, and ran for about five months. The reviews were sensational, but only the magazines and weeklies came. The papers refused to come because it wasn't an Equity theatre. The audiences were small, but consistent. I want to quote here two reviews we received: the first because he understood what we were trying to do, and the second because she loved us.

A mime show with music, presented by and at the Noble Path Theatre, 498 Third Ave. Directed by Richmond Shepard. By Arthur Sainer
Is the function of a mime to demonstrate the discipline of miming in the most excellent fashion possible, or is the function of the discipline to act as a vessel carrying an idea not necessarily peculiar to mime? I've not seen the latest Marcel Marceau, but his early pieces usually left me with the thought, "How beautifully he does it"—except for his "ages of man" piece, which said, in the most concise and marvelous fashion, "This is man's life." Most of his other pieces, though they dealt with specific situations, were really abstract exercises in which the discipline far outweighed the idea, e.g., man shoving an icebox, man watching a butterfly, man wandering through the park chucking babies under the chin, etc. How beautifully he did them. But do the standards for music and for abstract art hold true for mime, that the value is contained in the execution? Can this ever be true for a narrative art?

138

No One Way

The answer, probably, is that there is no one superior way of attacking mime, that the creator simply goes with his current impulse. But the question was engendered by the approach of Richmond Shepard, a vastly different approach from that of the early Marceau and Tony Montanaro and an extension of the early work of Jean-Louis Barrault. The Barrault that I've been exposed to dealt with highly dramatic and romantic material, was concerned with arousing a specific emotion in us for his symbolic and usually forlorn people. Pierrot, for example. Shepard is not concerned about arousing particular emotions for a particular character. Instead, by placing an ensemble on stage and having them mime the foibles of both primitive and sophisticated man, he is able to convey the full scale of our possibilities as particular creatures and as a culture. Thus we participate in an act of understanding rather than an act of feeling. Shepard gives us a psychic landscape, he offers us a set of beliefs. The mime as a discipline definitely is not there for its own sake.

Life Cycle

I was quite pleased by what I saw. Shepard seems almost obsessed by the notion of the life cycle, both of man and of civilization. Remember Spengler's notion of a "culture" degenerating into a "civilization"? That's here, the degeneration coming through man's turning into a specialist and losing his sense of the whole. So is the picture of man rising from the slime and learning the astonishing facts of his body. So is the picture of man during the stages of peace and war.

Many lovely things transpire on stage. There is a bit featuring a skull which is called "Discovery in the Inner-Temple" and deals with man attaining the tragic vision. Hallie Goodman does an exquisite solo as she depicts the life cycle of a woman from childhood to old age—identical in intent to Marceau's "ages of man," but beautiful nonetheless. And Jerry Santini creates a number of absorbing and disturbing perversions. And there are some quite funny moments—Shepard as an infinite variety of people, Shepard driving an automobile. And the music, partly improvised and performed by a trio consisting of Konrad Kaufman, Lucas Mason, and Michael Lobel on percussion, a trumpet, guitar, bass, and bamboo flute, was for me alone worth the evening.
In fact, I liked the whole company: Linda Eskenas, Paula Mason, David Cole, Annemarie Polonyi and Peter McGee.

This next review, by the New York correspondent of the **London Evening Standard** appeared in the Beaverbrook chain of papers all over the world:

Evening Standard, May 15, 1963
JEAN CAMPBELL
NEW YORK NEWSLETTER

NEW FORM

What holds people to New York? It is a city without love. A place to come to, to exploit and to leave. A city to live in, but never to die in. And yet, suddenly, you come upon things here—that grow out of the ugliness and savagery and hate that have infinite beauty.

I found such a thing in a tiny theatre two storeys up on Third Avenue and 33rd Street where a young man named Richmond Shepard has formed a troupe of mimers.

Using the music of percussion, trumpet, bamboo flutes and guitar, they perform a cyclical history of mankind. Richmond, who studied under Marcel Marceau—but leaves him as far behind as the Bluebird left the bicycle—says: "I believe that communication today demands no rules of established form. Whatever is needed to communicate with an audience—music, costume, even narration with the mime—is valid."

The result is a masterpiece that leaves anything I have seen in the theatre far behind. The giants like Brecht and Genet seem like the mutterings of a broken gramophone record after the impact of this new form of theatre.

Shepard has called his theatre the "Noble Path." Unlike most of our generation he has said, and thank heaven somebody has said it at last, "We believe in reaching towards the nobleness inherent in man's nature rather than in futility and degradation."

139

We received mail on that one from all over the world. I sent copies of both reviews to the New York daily papers, but no one came. We played every Thursday, Friday, and Saturday night, changing and improving week after week. We felt we had built a better mousetrap, but no one was beating any path to our door. Toward the end of the run Harry Breitman joined the cast, and one of the girls, Linda Eskenas, left to join Juki Arkin's mime troupe. There was a good feeling in the theatre—most of us were doing the Subud spiritual exercise, and there was a good, quiet, peaceful feeling in the atmosphere. Several people saw the show and stayed to talk with us afterward, and then joined Subud. Joseph Chaiken, an actor and theatre innovator, was one. Several people, including our stage manager, David Kitely, were living in the theatre, and somehow I was supporting my family from it. When spring ended, the Building Department decided that even though a theatre and/or acting studio had been operating on the premises for many years, and the fire department had passed us, there was some kind of mistake in the initial filing in 1916 on the building, and we had to close down. The man came twice, said he loved the show, but we had to close. We thought he wanted a bribe, but we had no money for one, so we closed.

The next year I worked as the M.C. for the Hootenanies at the Bitter End Cafe, and we appeared on the "Hootenany" television show. We did some college concerts, worked in the mountains during the summer, and as the year ended I went on relief and stayed on for about five months, until I got another show going. The welfare people didn't ask me to try any work but my own, and we got extra food from the federal government. Fortunately, I'm a good borrower, and so we got by. I had two daughters by now. My mother in California and father in New York didn't always agree with me, but they always helped out when they could.

In spring 1964 the owner of the Cafe Au GoGo on Bleeker Street, across from the Bitter End, decided it would be a good idea to put a mime theatre in the little shop above his club. I started casting. We found a stage manager, and built the stage, put in the lights and dimmer I had salvaged from Third Avenue, and started performing. The Buildings Department closed us—the place couldn't get a license. Paula Scott, one of the co-owners of The Actor's Playhouse, introduced me to a wonderful woman of the theatre, Jay Stanwyck, who had produced several off-Broadway shows, and Jay became our producer. We opened at The Actor's Playhouse in Sheridan Square, with Hallie Goodman, Daniel Landau, and Lily Tomlin doing the mime with me, my old friend Richard Gilden came from California and did the narration, and we had Lynn Cushman on flute, and Alan de Mause, who composed the music, on guitar. Eric Gertner stage managed.

This show was a little different from "Move Up!" There were only four mimes instead of eight, and for the first time we did improvisations as part of the show. In the second act, we had the audience call out objects, characters, or situations, and we improvised. There were also a couple of new pieces, and some of the old. Rosalind Zaman had designed beautiful color slides for us, and we projected them as background and sometimes onto the actors. We also used a movies projector in one spot. The show was exciting, the magazine reviewers agreed with me, and so did the TV reviewers. The newspapers hated it. An angry ninny from the **Post,** called Jerry Tallmer, saw only the first half, and wrote a scathing personal attack on me, telling me to give up trying to be Marcel Marceau, and one of the weeklies said the show was the best summertime entertainment in New York City. We closed in two weeks. There was no shock to it this time, though. You build calluses. I knew I had to go on doing what I do regardless of what some insensitive idiot wrote.

Jay lost the money she had put into the show, which was called "World of Illusion," and Weston and I worked in the mountains again.

It was at this point that I changed my first name. Richmond was received mystically as being a name that corresponds to the entity that inhabits my body better than the old name. It is the direction I have to go in. I've been using it for over five years now, and it feels better. Weston got his name the same way. We did the Today Show, mentioned the name of an airline, and got two free round-trip tickets to Europe, where we went to see the spiritual leader of Subud, who received the names for us. Weston stayed in Europe for four years; I stayed eight days. When I returned, I found that Doug and Kari Hunt's book, **Panto-mime—The Silent Theatre** had just been published by Atheneum, and they called me "America's foremost mime," under the old name.

Christmas 1964 I did my last New York show, "A Storyteller's Scrapbook," at the 4th Street Playhouse. Alice Knick, a friend of Jay Stanwyck, produced it, and we played for kids in the daytime. There were just three in the cast—one girl and me, sometimes it was Paula Mason, but usually Hallie Goodman, and Biff Rose played the banjo and narrated. This was the first time I used the name Richmond. (Yes, I did change it in copying the reviews a couple of pages ago.) That fall and winter I worked with Herb Gart, learning the theatrical personal management business, and learned that it wasn't for me. We managed Buffy

St. Marie, Patrick Sky, Hamilton Camp, Jesse Colin Young (of The Young-bloods), Mississippi John Hurt, Jim and Jean, and Biff Rose. Herb had good taste.

Summer 1965 I was hired to go to Cleveland to direct musicals at the Cain Park Playhouse, a 3,000-seat outdoor theatre, and to teach mime. We closed up our New York apartment, and made a detour to Los Angeles, where I had been hired to write the screenplay of a movie, **Noon on Doomsday,** based on a play of Rod Serling's on a civil rights theme. I had three daughters by now. My wife loved California, and we decided to move there after Cleveland. When I finished **Noon on Doomsday,** Jack Broder hired me to rewrite a science fiction film he was doing, called **The Navy versus the Night Monsters. Noon on Dooms-day** was shelved after I finished it because the producer, Marc Miller, couldn't get it financed, but Broder's film was made, with Mamie Van Doren and Anthony Eisley in the leads. Then Steve Allen read **Noon . . .** and hired me to write a film for him. We went to Cleveland, I directed **The Sound of Music** and **Brigadoon,** taught mime, wrote for Steve, and finally quit. We found Cleveland quite provincial, and Cain Park unrewarding, and I felt I should be in California where a lot was happening. We moved to Los Angeles, I finished the film for Steve Allen, and after a year here, I started teaching at several colleges. At thirty-seven I finally went to work, and signed year-long contracts to teach. I performed on "I Spy," "Occasional Wife," "That Girl," "The Second Hundred Years," "Good Morning World," "The Steve Allen Show," "The Donald O'Connor Show," and others.

When I taught in New York, it was haphazard—we did what I felt like doing that day. Now I had to make up a syllabus, so I gradually formulated the teaching sequence outlined in this book. I tried to give a new secret each week—some review, but always something new. When writing the exercises down for the pamphlet I put out, which this book is based on, I began to realize how many of the exercises I had invented. Over the years it had been necessary to find ways to show illusions, and using the basics that I had learned from others, I invented many of the physical moves you'll be doing.

After living in L.A. a couple of years, I heard about Theatre Games from Severn Darden and Avery Schreiber. I formed a company: Willy Switkes came from New York, Rusdi Lane joined us, and Stefanianna Christopherson and Bill Callaway, who were students of mine at The Los Angeles Civic Light Opera's Musical Theatre Workshop, and Joan Payne; Louis Schuman played bass, and Latif Allen played piano. We called ourselves "The L.A. Cabaret," Avery showed me the games, which were all created by Viola Spolin, and are outlined in her book, **Improvisation for the Theatre,** and we've been doing Theatre Games here and there ever since. We've done Theatre Games shows in night clubs, at colleges, two summers we did them in the Los Angeles parks. The show is always different—we never repeat: The audience is in at the moment of creation, and no one will ever see that material again. It's the most exciting theatre I've done. There's more latitude in it when mimes do it, so naturally I try to use people who can do both. Stefanianna has been the leading lady of the mime troupe for three years now, and then the L.A. Cabaret Troupe has included her, Lewis Arquette, Carol O'Leary, Nola Roeper, Susan Dahlstrom, Geoff Edwards, and Weston.

Summer of 1967 I met Les Crane, and he agreed to perform in a movie I had in mind, for no money. During that year I put the project together, and with the help of lots of professional people in Subud, we did it. We filmed during the summer of 1968, with Stefanianna co-starring, and Rupert Crosse, a fine actor who I had directed in his first role about seventeen years earlier, co-starring; Hamilton Camp, Rusdi Lane, and all the gang are in it. At this writing, we've just finished the editing, music recording, etc., and are hoping for a summer 1971 release. I wrote, produced, and directed, and was production manager and second cameraman.

So I've taught at Cal State, L.A., (and picked up a Masters Degree there) at Cal Western University in San Diego for three years, the Pasadena Playhouse for one year, The Musical Theatre Workshop for four years, and now Immaculate Heart College. We just did twenty-five mime shows at The Seattle Center Playhouse over Christmas 1969 and New Year's 1970 with Nola Roeper, Susan Dahlstrom, Don McLeod, and Albert Hall, with Corky Greene doing music and narration—good reviews and full houses.

So I'm forty, and again a new year is starting. What do I want to do in the future? I'd like to do a film once a year, Theatre Games on television regularly, and mime in a theatre a couple of months of the year. My next film will be about a mime. In this short bio, I've sort of listed events, rather than go into detail. Each event had lots of stories and feelings, but this is, after all, a book on the technique of mime, not on my life. That'll come later, maybe. Meanwhile, I sometimes remember the voice of Lord Buckley, which came to me in a dream several years after his death, saying: "Have courage, Great Warrior!"

RICHMOND SHEPARD, who has been called America's foremost mime, studied mime in Paris with Marcel Marceau and Etienne Decroux. In 1952, he began his first mime troupe with an ensemble production of poems by A. A. Milne at the Circle in the Square in New York's Greenwich Village. That same year he started giving classes in mime. Shepard has been teaching and performing ever since. He has appeared on numerous television shows, has directed short and feature-length films, and has directed theatre pieces across the country, including productions in his native New York, where he has received three theatre awards. Shepard has a Ph.D. in communication, and has taught mime at Princeton University, The Living Theatre, Pasadena Playhouse, California State College/Los Angeles, and the University of Southern California. Currently, he teaches at his own studio in Hollywood and performs in theatres and at colleges and universities throughout the United States.

Photograph by David Cantrell